Journal of a Prairie Year

Journal of a Prairie Year

PAUL GRUCHOW

milkweed
editions

Published 2009 by Milkweed Editions
First published by the University of Minnesota Press in 1985
Printed in Canada
Cover design by Frances Baca
Cover photo by Duncan Walker
Interior design by Connie Kuhnz
Interior photographs by Joe Rossi
The text of this book is set in Goudy Old Style.
09 10 11 12 13 5 4 3 2 1
Second Edition

Please turn to the back of this book for a list
of the sustaining funders of Milkweed Editions.

ISBN 978-1-57131-318-8

The Library of Congress has catalogued the previous edition of this book as follows:

Gruchow, Paul.

    Journal of a prairie year.
    Bibliography: p.
    1. Northwestern States—Description and travel.   2. Prairie
Provinces—Description and travel.   3. Natural history—North-
western States.   4. Natural history—Prairie Provinces.   5. Gruchow,
Paul—Diaries. I. Title
    F597.G82 1985   9 17.8'0433   85-16493
    ISBN 0-8166-1425-3
    ISBN 0-8166-1426-1 (pbk.)

Journal of a Prairie Year

Foreword
Scott Russell Sanders

At the beginning of the nineteenth century, travelers setting out from the southern lip of Lake Michigan, where Chicago sprawls today, could have rolled westward to the Rocky Mountains through an uninterrupted sea of grass. By midsummer in the eastern reaches of this vast prairie, they wouldn't have been able to see over the waving bluestem as they waded through Indian grass, switchgrass, coneflowers, sunflowers, blazing stars, goldenrods, wild indigos, and hundreds of other species of plants. This swath of tallgrass prairie stretched north and south in a sinuous belt more than a thousand miles long. In the north, travelers would have found all the water they needed in potholes, ponds, and lakes. Along the winding rivers, they would have found enough cottonwoods and willows for shelter and fire. And everywhere they would have found an abundance of game, for these grasslands nourished immense herds of bison, as well as antelope, deer, rabbits, geese, and ducks.

By the mid-twentieth century, when Paul Gruchow was growing up in southwestern Minnesota, the tallgrass prairie that had once nurtured big bluestem and bison had become little more than a memory. All but a few remnants of these millions of acres had been plowed or paved; creeks had been straightened into ditches; potholes had been drained; vast herds and flocks had dwindled or entirely disappeared. "It is by now a pale ghost of the world that once existed in this place," Gruchow writes, for he knew how much luxuriance had been lost, and this knowledge runs like a lament through these pages. But he also knew, from close observation, how much energy and beauty still welled up from these prairie soils, how much power rode on the winds, how much glory shone from the skies. And so we find in *Journal of a Prairie Year*, the first of several marvelous books by Paul Gruchow, the testament of a man who simultaneously aches and rejoices over the land he calls home.

Shaping a book around the cycle of the seasons is a venerable device, exemplified in American nature writing most famously by *Walden* and *A Sand County Almanac*. However, as it was for Henry David Thoreau and Aldo Leopold, this choice of form went far beyond mere literary strategy for Paul Gruchow—it was a way of situating human experience within greater-than-human patterns. And the study of these deeper patterns, what we call "natural history," is the history that counts, for it is our attempt at understanding the living matrix that embraces and ultimately constrains all of our actions. Rachel Carson spoke of this truth when she said: "If we have ever regarded our interest in natural history as an escape from the realities of our modern world, let us now reverse this attitude. For the mysteries of living things, and the birth and death of continents and seas, are among the great realities" (*Lost Woods*, Beacon Press, 1999).

Gruchow was not much interested in the "modern world" of machines, stock markets, and cities, but he was fascinated by "the great realities" of nature. Whether describing thunderstorms or birdsongs, night skies awash with stars or puddles awash with tadpoles, dragonflies darting or garter snakes mating, he illustrates on every page his claim that "the mystery has captivated me, and under the spell of it, I have meandered, like the drifts of snow, across the wide prairies."

Despite decades of plowing and paving, those wide prairies are still poor in what geologists call "relief," the ups and downs provided elsewhere by hills and valleys, mountains and canyons. Many observers, lacking Gruchow's attentiveness, confuse this flatness of terrain with a lack of interest, and some attribute the same quality to those who live there, especially on farms or in small towns. Gruchow suffered no such misconceptions, for he had looked patiently enough to see the richness and resilience of both the people and the place. He was a champion not only of the "great realities" of the prairie but also of those who dwell there, as he did, out of affection rather than inertia.

Yet he also knew that the expanse and indifference of the grasslands could drive its inhabitants to "prairie madness" and, in extreme cases, suicide. For all creatures on the prairie, he remarks, "the condition of life is to be hunted," whether by predators or by loneliness. In this *Journal,* he notes the loneliness he had felt while growing up on a hardscrabble farm in southwestern Minnesota and the remnant sense of isolation that would haunt him until the end of his life. Those who have followed Paul Gruchow's career realize that the end came too early, as he took his own life at the age of 56 after battling severe depression for years. The prairie did not cause his illness, which ran in his family, but this challenging terrain may have offered him a way of imagining his tumultuous inner landscape.

Despite his struggles, Gruchow never despaired of nature. Although "death was always lurking in the shadows," life kept breaking through. Indeed, shortly after he acknowledges the prairie madness that drives some to desperate ends, he describes "a high-flying wedge of snow geese heading north at midwinter. . . . Their high-spirited honking drifted down to earth. They flew on another mile and suddenly descended to earth in a squabble of confusion. There was silence again. But the fact of the wind and the cold had somehow been taken away." The spectacle of a badger sliding down a grassy slope leads him to conclude that "it is impossible to listen to a coyote singing at moonrise or to watch a flock of swallows on the wing or to encounter a young badger at play without believing that joy is as much a biological fact of life as any other. I, at any rate, catching the mood of the badger, went on my way again with a skip and a hop." That seems a fitting image to carry away of this keen-eyed observer, who relished every sign of wildness in his home ground, and invited his reader to feel the same joy in life.

Near the end of this eloquent book he proclaimed himself to be, utterly and forever, "a prairie person." Although his homeland had been reduced to a ghost of its former self, the natural forces that had created the tallgrass prairie were still at play. And for Paul Gruchow, the sun and soil, the wind and rain, and the exuberance of living things were the enduring realities.

Journal of a Prairie Year

Prologue

I drove from the southern border of Minnesota to Winnipeg. The drive carried me from the heart of the old tallgrass prairie to its northern edge. Beyond Winnipeg, the boreal forests of the subarctic shield take hold. Altogether, I traveled more than 600 miles northward, every mile of the distance a deeper excursion into the dimensions of flatness.

The route I chose was through the eastern Dakotas. It was in late afternoon, when the light is at its most dramatic, that I approached Sisseton, South Dakota. A prairie coteau runs that way. On a topographical map it doesn't look like much: a thin and rather random scratch of brown on a tan plate. And in fact there aren't any obstructions to the view, no foothills, no forests, no man-made monuments, this being country in which acquiring a mobile home is stepping up in the world.

The coteau presented itself unadorned. For a time, I was not aware that I was approaching it. Then it seemed to surround me on all sides; I had the sensation of driving in a gigantic dish. Then I had achieved the top of the coteau, and I could see so far across the prairie that the brown earth looked blue at the edges of the horizon. My ears popped on the way down from Sisseton to Fargo, North Dakota.

I have climbed up to mountaintops and down from them. I know that going to the coteau is going to a mountaintop, and I know that coming down from the coteau is coming down from a mountaintop. I cannot explain why this landscape seems so flat.

It is flat, I suppose, as the deserts are flat, as the oceans are flat, as the polar ice caps are flat. It is flat because of the immensity of its distances. And it is flat as a grain of sand is flat to a person who owns no microscope.

What seems flat seems empty. When we are faced with vastness on the scale of the prairie, we turn inward. "One might say," the French philosopher Gaston Bachelard wrote, "that immensity is a philosophical category of daydream."

The prairie is like a daydream. It is one of those plainly visible things that you can't photograph. No camera lens can take in a big enough piece of it. The prairie landscape embraces the whole of the sky. Its image is globular, but without the distortion you get in a wide-angle lens. Any undistorted image is too flat to represent the impression of immersion that is central to being on the prairie. The experience is a kind of baptism.

The moon is the closest of the celestial objects; it makes the largest image; it affords the best light for prolonged examination; it is visible in the greatest detail. But no amount of walking will get you any closer to it, and you can't reach out and touch it. The prairie, in this respect, resembles the moon. The essential feature of the prairie is its horizon, which you can neither walk to nor touch. It is like the horizon of the sea.

We are helpless as babies about this. Whatever we can see and do not understand and must acknowledge, we make over in our own image. The moon, the sea, the prairie—all present insurmountable barriers of distance. We cross them on the craft of egocentricity. We make the moon the marker of time and the dwelling place of desire; the sea the mirror, the bosom; the prairie the breadbasket.

Newcomers to the prairie are at first disconcerted by its nakedness. Later, they will wish it weren't so private.

To live on the prairie is to daydream. It is the only conceivable response to such immensity. It is when we are smallest that our daydreams come quickest. I drove north across the prairie daydreaming and taking notes. When I got to Winnipeg, my notes stopped.

Downtown Winnipeg is everything that the open prairie is not. Swirls of unruly traffic. Swarms of pedestrians. Towering masses of glass and steel. If you don't scurry about, you make a nuisance of yourself and invite attention as a person apparently without gainful employment.

I stayed in the big railroad hotel downtown. The second morning I was in Winnipeg, I was intimidated by the rush of traffic into making a wrong turn, and before I realized what I had done, I was out of the city. Figuring I might as well enjoy being lost, I turned off onto a road that promised to lead through the countryside. By and by, I happened upon Lower Fort Garry, which was once a provisioning outpost of the Hudson Bay Company and is now a kind of Williamsburg, a restored historical site in which costumed students enact life from another time. It was a blustery and chilly day. I was glad to be inside the walls. A young cook in a bonnet offered me a still-warm, coals-baked oatmeal cookie. I was emboldened by it to venture out through the gates of the fort and stand, clutched against a tree, along the banks of the Red River of the North. The wind howled. Even the gulls seemed to be having a hard time of it.

I went back to Winnipeg through marginal farmlands along what was once the bottom of a great sea. I had no trouble finding the city. It loomed out of the landscape like an enormous tree. I saw the city then as a fortress. I saw what walls we build against the prairie, how timidly we huddle together, how effectively we close off its vastness of space and make for ourselves another space of more human proportions.

I couldn't say what to make of it. I drove the 600 miles home through rain, through mist, through sunshine. What I saw in every light until I was obsessed with seeing it was that nearly every inch of land along the way had been painstakingly turned over, furrow by furrow. It seemed some unknowable comment on the human spirit that we should, despite our walls, have turned ourselves into such an awesome army of Lady Macbeths, rubbing out so relentlessly such a terrible space.

Winter

1

In January came the sting of hard winter, of polar winds, of driven snow, of sunshine without warmth.

The little winter birds—the chickadees, the juncos, the nut-hatches—gathered at the backyard feeders and ate and shivered. They survived the handicaps of the weather and of their own tiny bodies by, among other strategies, eating and shivering. The birds that survived would shiver until the first warm day of spring.

The squirrels, so inconspicuous in summer, perched on the limbs of bald trees, their tails draped forward over their backs. The crows had given up calling to each other in the mornings and the evenings.

I sat one winter night in a town café listening to a farmer talk about the surprisingly complex language of pigs. The farmer said that simply from the sound of a pig, one could with experience tell its age, its approximate weight, and what had prompted it to cry out, whether it was being stepped on, or denied mother's milk, or whatever. He and his wife, the farmer said, had once occupied themselves during a long drive in cataloging the number of pig expressions they knew, and they had made a list of fifty before their journey had come to an end.

I am not a raiser of pigs. I cannot tell one pig noise from another. But I am a walker, and it occurred to me that it can be said in the same sense that the snow speaks. With proper attention, one can learn to tell the temperature of the air, the depth of snowfall on the ground, and the condition of the weather in the preceding week from the sound of snow underfoot.

By sound of foot against snow, one can tell the powdery snows of early winter from the wet snows of late winter, and both of them from the denser, harder snows of high winter.

One can tell the crunch of snow against foot on a day of more than 20°F from the squeak of snow on a day of 0°, and both from the hollow moan of the snow on a subzero day. One can distinguish by the sound of it the thin snow of open places from the drifted snow of sheltered places.

The deep snow of the first of January does not sound at all like the crusted snow after the thaw of early February. The Objibwe, in fact, named the months for the differences between the two: first there was the Moon of the Deep Snow and then the Moon of the Crusted Snow.

Are the sounds of the snow based on differences in crystalline structure? I have never seen this worked out anywhere. Snow crystals, with sometimes six, sometimes three, sometimes five sides, form in hexagonal plates at temperatures from 28°F to freezing; in needles from 24° to 27°; in hollow prismatic columns from 19° to 23°; in another kind of hexagonal plate from 11° to 18°; in fernlike stars from 4° to 10°; in plates again from −13° to 3°; and again in hollow prismatic columns at temperatures below −13°.

There is some principle of physics at work in the music of snow underfoot, just as there is a mathematical principle to explain why snow drifts at a fenceline in a scalloped pattern of elongated ovals rather than in the straight line of the fence. It does so for the same reason that a river meanders rather than advances in a straight line. I cannot explain the mathematics involved any more than I can articulate the structural underpinnings of the music of snow underfoot.

If I could explain the sound of a footstep upon the snow or come to know the underlying principles that govern the meandering of the snow along a fenceline, I should then be attuned in a new way to the largely unheard and mysterious music of the universe. It has often been said, and I shall argue the case myself, that the only remark of nature is its silence, but that is not because the world around us has nothing to say. It is because we come unequipped with ears to hear.

I am as unequipped as the next person. I listen in the dead of winter to the song the snow sings, and strain as I might, I cannot make it out. I listen to the coyotes howling in the nights and to the crows cawing in the mornings and to the wind washing in the leaves of the cottonwoods in the evenings, and I know that I have not really heard anything of it except the mystery in it. But the mystery has captivated me, and under the spell of it, I have meandered, like the drifts of snow, across the wide prairies.

2

The winter sky is the plain and homely sister of the skies, the sad-sack one, the ash sky, all gray and featureless, pale in the morning, pale at noon, pale at night. The winter sunrises are late and boringly pastel, and the sunsets are early and boringly pastel.

The earth in winter stares blankly back at the cold and featureless sky, does nothing to enhance or mimic it. Even the stars in winter do not seem to sparkle as they do at other times of the year.

I was driving through Minneapolis one winter night with my five-year-old daughter. She looked out of her window and spied the moon. "Oh!" she exclaimed. "That's why we haven't been having a moon at home. It's been up here in Minneapolis!"

She stared at the moon in silence for a long time. "The moon looks so sad in winter," she said. She stared up at the moon a while longer. "No wonder it's so sad," she said at last. "It doesn't even have any stars to keep it company."

The winter sky does, however, have its moments. They are the moments at dusk or at dawn when the angle of the light is exactly right to catch the crystalline haze in the air. Then the sun can be seen to be crowned with a halo or bracketed by sun dogs, and sometimes these dogs are as brilliantly multicolored as the rainbows that follow the summer rains. Or the sun seems just at the moment of setting to take the shape of a Roman cross, belled at the bottom and luminescent. It is on such nights that the lights of the little prairie towns stretch up into the sky like searchlights. Every settlement seems surrounded then by its private show of Northern Lights.

And there are the dawns and the dusks when the snow is falling, when the lights in the villages take on a fat and gauzy glow, when the whole prairie world, although dark, seems somehow aglow, when the sky above the storm becomes the particular pale pink of a prairie rose in bloom. When the winter sky puts on that face, the only possible response is to keep silent, as before any many-splendored thing.

3

It was a bright, mild, sparkling morning in early February. There was scarcely a breeze. There had been a snowfall six days earlier. The road to the quarry showed the tracks of the rabbits that had run there, but there was no sign of the humans who flocked to the place at any other time of year. Even in its prettiest dress, winter attracts scant notice.

Birds were singing everywhere in the thicket of trees at the base of the cliff. Half a dozen chickadees smartly capped in black jockeyed for places on the limbs of an oak tree. A crow passed overhead.

Beneath the trees, there was a place among the talus where the passing animals had traveled so frequently on one kind of business or another that a smooth, firm path had been worn in the snow.

On a little ledge in the face of the cliff rested the frozen carcass of a spider, one of thousands of casualties of the season in that place.

Atop the cliff, the isolated blond tufts of buffalo grass stood in the cracks of red rocks, each tuft bundled in white snow. The bunches of dried blue grama grass, a survivor in the harshest and driest of places, nodded their long eyelashes.

Where the high prairie had been burned in the fall before, the landscape was black and barren, but where the grasses still stood, the landscape was covered with a soft, loose blanket of snow. It was one of the services that the dense sod performed for all the plants on the prairie: to catch and save the precious snow to feed the burst of new growth in the spring.

There were fewer footprints on high than in the valley below: signs of deer, of a fox, of a rabbit, of a mouse, of a shrew perhaps pregnant by now, and they were widely scattered.

No birds sang. The grasses did not rustle. There was no buzzing of insects. And no croaking of frogs at the stock ponds. Even the farm implements were silent.

In the summer, everything in this place seemed to quiver with the continuous wavering of a thousand songs and sounds. But on this day, the quavering had stopped, and a clear, bright calm had descended and had covered everything with its sweet peace.

4

The blue light of the full moon, the Moon of the Crusted Snow, was already beginning to wane.

Talcot Lake. Midafternoon. The glare of sun on snow was blinding. It was necessary to make a shade with your hands to see into the distance.

In the open, the snow was packed hard enough to hold the weight of a human. In some spots, it was so hard that the hooves of the passing deer had not completely penetrated it. But in the woods, the snow was soft and deep, and walking was nearly impossible except on the numerous paths the deer had made in their extensive yard. Everywhere there were icy ruts where deer had bedded down and melted the snow with the warmth of their bodies.

I stood in the shadow of an uprooted tree at the edge of the lake and watched and listened.

Beyond the tall plumes of the *Phragmites*, there seemed at first to be no life. Then one deer stepped out onto the lake, and two, then deer were apparent everywhere, standing along the lakeshore, among the cattail rushes, on the hillsides, in the fields and woods beyond the lake. The lake seemed suddenly to be as alive with the motion of deer as an anthill is with the business of ants on a hot day in August. Then I became aware of a spot of brown at midlake. I realized I was seeing a red fox and that the fox was stalking some invisible quarry.

The deer in the farther distance were, like me, at a standstill. They were gathered in groups, their ears up, their heads high, watching the hunt of the fox too. The fox seemed oblivious to the spectacle it was creating.

It stole forward. Forward a little more. Suddenly, a pair of ducks, the objects of the fox's quest, took to the air with a clamor and headed north to a quieter place. Their quacks grew fainter and fainter.

The fox pursued them for a few yards, stopped, looked sheepish, turned, and loped easily across the lake, passed through the crowds of onlooking deer, and disappeared around a bend in the shoreline.

Now a second fox appeared, a second watcher in the wings. It soon turned and ran away too.

The deer began to move again. They came in a steady stream out of the woods and onto the surface of the lake. There seemed to be no end to them.

I thought of the profusion of life that had once teemed upon the prairies: great herds of bison, pronghorn antelopes by the millions, clouds of locusts that blackened the skies, waterfowl in spring and fall settling on hundreds of sloughs by the tens of thousands.

A few of the deer moved around a bed of reeds, passed the dam, and came to within a hundred yards of me. The small doe leading the way was frisky. She seemed to leap for the pleasure of leaping, prancing rather than running. She danced her way across the ice. Then she spied me. She stopped short. She assessed the potential for danger, decided to move ahead. When she did, the frisk had gone out of her step. She ran swiftly in high, bounding leaps.

I watched as she sailed into the cattails. Her white tail was up all the way. It waved back and forth like a flag of truce after the rest of her body had disappeared from view.

Silence again.

In a tree overhead, a bird began to sing a homely little song on a high, short, scraping note, like the sound of a door hinge squeaking.

Now and then the bird tapped the bark of the tree for small morsels of food. It was like the sound of a carpenter at work in the distance. A second bird began the same song and set up the same tapping. They were the birds that work trees upside down, the birds with the patrician beaks, the white-breasted nuthatches.

The sun came down a little, and the sky began to color. The shadows grew long and sharp. I followed the highway up the frozen river toward home.

At the dam, I paused at the place where the water was still open and saw carp gathered in great numbers to suck up the oxygen that the stagnant water itself no longer adequately supplied. They were crowded together, scale to scale. They did not so much move as writhe. Some of them were already dead, and their white bellies showed brilliantly on the surface of the water against the black backs of the fish that still lived.

As I watched, one of the carp began to list in the water, came up once or twice to the surface for air, turned a time or two onto its side, got right again, finally, too weak to fight for survival, turned up on its belly, feebly fluttered its fins, and expired.

I went up the river. At the last bend, I came upon the carcass of a yearling doe, exceedingly small of stature and thin, that had laid down beneath a willow tree to rest and had never awakened. I admired the deer on my knees, lifted its stiff head in my hands, looked into its fixed eyes, the color of frozen cream, left it behind.

It was the dawn of the new year, the coldest hour of the day, the hour when babies come, when the rattle of death sounds.

5

A road led a good part of the way around Rush Lake. It came in from the highway, crossed the railroad tracks, and went down to the boat landing; from there, it followed the edge of the marsh as far as the spring in one direction, as far as the outlet in the other. The road was little more than a dirt track. It was a mire of mud in the spring, a puddle of dust by midsummer, and by this time of the winter, it had drifted impassably full of snow. The snow had been packed by a dozen hard winds, and it had settled on melting days and crusted over on colder ones. It was now as easy to walk across as a city sidewalk.

Even on its passable days, the road attracted little traffic. Now and then, an angler came in the summer and put a boat in at the landing. A few hunters came down in the fall to try their sights at the migrating waterfowl.

There was a bit of bank along the edge of the lake. On top of it stood towering cottonwood trees, and beneath these, a thicket of plums. The whole of it was, even in the barrenness of winter, a nearly impenetrable tangle. In the unseemly thicket of cottonwoods and plums at the edge of the marsh there was evidence of abundant life even in high winter. One could see the paths and markings of many rabbits, the foot and body prints of deer, the trailings of many small rodents, the tracks of pheasants and of a host of smaller birds, the stripped cobs of field corn that squirrels had carried back to their perches in the cottonwoods, the signs of a weasel. The tracks converged at a spring, where open water ran almost all year round, and the road that separated the thicket and the marsh from the cornfield had served, it was plain, as a highway for the whole animal community.

The place was an island of wildness in all the surrounding sea of domesticity. I approached it on foot. When I drew near, I saw that two deer stood as sentinels at the gate. They did not forbid me entry, but neither did they welcome me. They turned when I was at the last hundred yards across the cultivated stubble and disappeared silently into the wildness, their white tails flashing disrespect.

6

It has been to places like Rush Lake that I have repaired in every season of the year from the time when I was a young boy. I have been afflicted with wanderlust for as long as I can remember. It is the characteristic hunger of isolation.

I was born at mid-century. My parents, who were poor and rural, had never amounted to anything, and never would, and never expected to. They were rather glad for the inconsequence of their lives. They got up with the sun and retired with it. Their routines were dictated by the seasons. In summer they tended; in fall they harvested; in winter they repaired; in spring they planted. It had always been so; so it would always be.

The farmstead we occupied was on a hilltop overlooking a marshy river bottom that stretched from horizon to horizon. It was half a mile from any road and an eternity from any connection with the rest of the culture. There were no books there; there was no music; there was no television; for a long time, no telephone. Only on the rarest of occasions—a time or two a year—was there a social visitor other than the pastor. There was no conversation in that house.

The highest event of the year was the night in October when the tomcat who ruled the territory came. He came every October without fail. Like the pastor, the cat was always offered something to eat. In the cat's case, it was always a tin pie plate of goat's milk into which a thick slice or two of dense homemade bread had been crumbled. He was an enormous yellow cat with eyes the size of a horned owl's. Eventually all the other barn cats in the neighborhood came to look just like him. Nobody knew how many generations of kittens he had sired. He loved his goat's milk and his chunks of soggy bread. His purr filled the farmstead kitchen. He loved to be petted. After he had been fed, he spent an hour or more circling the little room, holding his tail high, arching his back, rubbing himself against our ankles. It was a kind of prenuptial dance. Then he would beg to be let out into the night, and it would be October again before he would return. We always stood in the doorway and watched him disappear across the yard.

One October, the cat didn't come back. Nobody ever saw him again. After that, there was a new degree of silence in our household.

I knew even as a young boy that I would not bear the silence. I ran away for the first time at eighteen months of age. I got a mile and a half. I was on a bridgetop mesmerized by the music of the water running into the drainage ditch below when the gasman found me and carried me home. I was soundly spanked. But there was no keeping me.

I was six or seven when I stopped wandering along the roads and started taking the back way to the wildernesses, to the fencerows, to the meadows, to the marshes, to the river.

I took a liking to bones, made a collection of them in the hayloft. I believed in ghosts, heard them in the night, saw their faces in the bald moonlit trunks of cottonwoods. It was the ghostliness in the bones that attracted me. I was indiscriminate about them. The pincers of crayfish were as satisfying to me as the femurs of cows.

There were mudholes in the meadows where cattle ran and these sometimes entrapped cows. The femurs, even the skulls, of cattle were available for the taking. I knew a place where there was a whole skeleton, picked clean by scavengers, lying white as a ghost and half-immersed in the muck. I visited it often as a boy and hoped to catch in the eerie silence of the place even something so compromised as the half-wild spirit of the creature who had died there.

Perhaps I did catch something of this spirit. My habit of collecting bones came to an end. I took up the trapping of the furbearers that lived in the river bottom. I learned to catch muskrats, skunks, and weasels. I subscribed to *Fur, Fish & Game*. I dreamed of living someday in a cabin in the Adirondacks. In these dreams, I was always alone, it was always winter, and I was always out on my snowshoes tending one of my traplines. It was an evergreen world, silent and unsullied.

I was not after the pelts, nor the money I got from selling them. I had to be nagged to skin the creatures I caught and to see to stretching the pelts and scraping and drying them. Once I had caught a creature, I was through with it.

I was after a share of the wildness in the creatures I was pursuing. I wanted the thrill of thinking like something wild, of guessing where I would be if I were, say, a weasel, of imagining the things that might then rouse my curiosity, of thinking just where I would step. I wanted to be able to read the landscape in the way that a weasel does, to share its habit of seeing, to assume its language. I was like a blind man imagining sight or a deaf man hearing. I yearned for that leap of imagination that would send me off into the unimaginable wildness.

The day came when I thought I might match wits against a mink, the smartest, the most elusive of the wild creatures I knew. I had spent years by now watching the life in my valley, but the mink was a creature of the night, and I had never chanced even to catch a glimpse of one. Nevertheless, I knew they existed, and I knew where. The signs of them, which I had learned to read, were all around.

My father showed me how to set a trap on a slide so that when I caught my mink, it would be quickly drowned. He showed me the basic principles of positioning a trap for a mink: how to follow the trail of the mink along a streambank, what sort of obstruction would force it down into the water, where it would be likely to move when it was so diverted, how to construct an artificial diversion, how to conceal a trap without demobilizing it, how to use a bit of musk oil as a come-on and where to apply it in relation to the trap. I followed my father's instructions and felt myself drawn nearer to the wildness I sought. I imagined that I was an Indian boy long ago and that the instruction I was getting was ultimately in the art of survival. I wished to need to know how to survive, as boys once did.

I set my traps and tended them. When they failed to produce, I made adjustments. Once or twice I found a sprung trap, and these gave me encouragement. But the mink remained elusive.

A new season came, and I set out my lines again. Every trap was aimed at a mink. I could not be bothered with such mundane matters as catching mere muskrats. I did catch two or three of them quite by accident that season, however. No mink.

One day near the end of the season, there was warning of a blizzard. My father told me to pull in my traps while I still could, but I ignored the advice. Before I could make a last check of them, the snow started to fall so heavily and the winds began to drive it so fiercely that there could be no thought of going down into the valley. The snow fell all that day and the next, and the wind blew for two nights and three days before there was peace again.

Midway through my rounds the next spring, at a set that had been sprung the preceding fall, I found a trap out of place. I yanked its stake up, and when I began to pull on its chain, I realized there was more than a trap at the other end of it. The little stream was swollen with the debris of the spring flood, and it was nasty business to get the catch untangled and up into the air. When the trap finally drew up, I saw that I had a mink on the end of it, a fine buck mink in a splendid dark winter coat. It was somewhat the worse for wear, having spent its winter in ice and its spring being bumped and scraped about in the muck of the melt, but it was still quite a prize.

I was wild with excitement. But when I unsnared it, I saw that my slide had not worked properly. The mink had not drowned right away. It had very nearly gnawed its leg through before death had come. I understood that the creature had been caught as that storm had come up. It had been intent upon finding shelter and a bit less wary than usual. It had made a desperate attempt to free itself, had nearly succeeded, and only the fact of the storm had finally done it in.

I took the mink home, skinned it, fleshed it, stretched it, hung it up to dry. The carcass I gave to the barn cats, which chewed it down to bones before the night was out. And then I took myself away to a private place and faced the sadness that had swollen up inside me. I did not understand it then or ever. The best I could make of it was that I was feeling a kind of shame for having taken advantage of the mink I had so admired. I could in a sense partake of its wildness; with enough patience and study I could make out its ways and deliver it into my own hands; I could learn the language of the wild mink. But the consequence was, and always would be, some kind of destruction.

From that day on, I put a distance between myself and the mink. I never again tried to trap it or any other creature. It was, I suppose, something of a denial of my own nature. Perhaps this was in itself a step back toward wildness.

After that it seemed as though I was always happening upon a mink somewhere. I saw mink many times even in daylight, always fleetingly. I would be passing around the shore of a lake or approaching the edge of a marsh or sitting in a tree somewhere, watching the spectacle all about, when out of the corner of my eye I would catch the dark blur of motion. A mink under these circumstances had a serpentine look:

low, furtive, fast-moving. It had always the manner of a creature just escaping from the scene of the crime. A time or two, I had even seen a mink crossing a highway in broad daylight, and once I had seen one on a city street in midafternoon, crouched down and running like hell from a bank robbery or something.

One springtime years later, I went down to the dam in Blue Mounds State Park to watch the annual migration of the carp. In the springtime, like the fabled salmon of the Northwest, the carp in the park's lower pond try to make their way up a tiny stream, over a dam, and into the upper pond. The height of the dam is six or eight feet above spring water level; it is an overwhelming barrier to a leaping carp. I have never seen one make it.

The length of the odds is nothing to discourage a carp. Time and time again, one will use the strength of its tail to throw itself up into the air. Generally, it will land upon the jagged rocks somwhere forward of the position from which it started. It will come down with a slap, and then either it will be washed back into the pool it started from, or it will be in a position to heave itself up into the air again and try its luck at another advance upon the waterfall. The efforts of an hour might bring it at last to the base of the concrete dam, where it will try again and again to leap up into the pond until, in tiredness or miscalculation, it makes a jump that causes it to fall out of range of the highest holding pool. Then it will slide and bang down into the stream again, from which it will mount a new assault on the pond.

I was there at the edge of the uppermost pond, altogether caught up in the ordeal of the carp, when I became aware, as one does by some sixth sense, that I was not alone. The tension of the second presence was palpable. I tried to see where the creature was, taking care not to make any grand or jagged movement that would alarm it. But I could see nothing.

A minute or two passed. A small carp almost at my feet made a feeble assault on the mountainous dam, failed, fell with a splash back into the pool. Momentarily stunned from the fall, it was taking a few seconds to get its sense of direction again. That hesitation proved fatal: a dark creature lunged forward, snared the fish in its claws, secured it behind the head in its jaws, and disappeared into the thicket of rushes at the edge of the holding pool. The whole action took a few seconds. It was like the brief shadow of a cloud passing.

I turned quickly, looked down the bank of the stream. In two spots where it was exposed, I saw the mink emerge with the fish in its mouth and disappear again into the young green vegetation. In a minute it was gone, forever out of sight. I spent a long time trying to trace it, to get another glimpse of it, to discover where it had gone with the fish, but the search came to nothing. It was as futile an effort as the one the vulnerable carp was making at the foot of the dam. Water fell over the dam and crashed down upon the rocks with a roar and ran off in the mysterious direction of the mink.

That was all there was to it. But the experience stayed with me. For at least those couple of minutes one springtime afternoon, the mink and I had stood side by side on the bank of that little stream, both fishing after the same object, in our unique ways. In that evanescence, we had been—however briefly, however tangentially—soul mates.

Now it was high winter on Rush Lake, and I was wandering again. The landscape was as clean and spare as any the prairie winter offers: signs of a mouse, here and there the tracks of a pheasant, at a few of the muskrat houses on the lake open breathing holes indicating residents, a pair of cottontail rabbits in the shelter of the shore, a shrike shouting from a treetop, a pair of chickadees, in the distance the calling of a crow. The wind had piled the snow in waves and scalloped them to look like the beached and empty shells of sea creatures. The waves of the lake itself had been caught and frozen in midair. Here not only sound but motion had been suspended.

And then, at midlake, the creature presented itself again. I had stopped at one of the largest muskrat houses to look for signs of occupancy. In the fresh snow around the rather large air hole, I saw the footprints of a mink. The mink had not entered the house. It had merely paused there to investigate; then it had urinated at the edge of the hole, dropped its scat, and gone on its way. The snow on the surface of the lake was older and harder-packed. In a few feet, the

trail of the mink disappeared. The droppings on the house were full
of muskrat hair.

I wandered until dusk, drinking in the sharpness, the cleanness of
the winter air. When the sun set, it was almost colorless, as under-
stated as everything else in winter, except for the wind.

I came out upon the road again and climbed a little knoll toward the
highway. The light was falling rapidly. The cars passing on the highway were already operating with headlights. And then in the shadows
ahead I saw the mink. It may have been the one I had seen signs of
earlier. The mink turned, stared at me for a long, deliberate second,
disappeared.

It was for all the world like a wink.

7

I collected a piece of cottonwood tree bark—it was a foot wide, two
and a half feet long, and an inch and a half deep—and carried it back
to my study. I let it sit there in the warmth of the room for a couple of
days. Then I got out my hand lens, cleared away the accumulation of
papers and books and scraps of gum wrapper from my table, and placed
the bit of bark before me to see what I could see.

I had collected the bark—a dead shell of cork in a dead season from
a tree that was forever dying—because I had expected to find some evidence of life in it. It would be my deceit, to work up wonder at the
paradox of life among the ruins. I would discover a teeming universe of
life in the mountains and canyons that had formed around the soft heart
of a tree growing in springwater at the edge of a prairie marsh. I would
make something of this discovery.

Even before I got down to work, before I polished my lens and as-
sembled my taxonomic keys, before I put myself into a frame of mind
receptive to wonderment, I was aware that my experiment was ca-
reening out of control. Little specks of things were already crawling
across my notepaper; something had taken wing and was loose in the
stale air of my study. A spider was dangling from the edge of my table
on a silk string. It threatened to lodge on my lap. I couldn't tell what

anything was: I was altogether at a loss for names of species, and the evidence was rapidly migrating beyond my reach before I could think what to do. There was a tickling sensation up the leg of my trousers. I was loathe to scratch lest the irritant be just what I was looking for. Nevertheless, I scratched and did not attempt to calculate the loss. It was possible that I was being mocked.

The outer surfaces of the bark were very nearly covered with two species of lichens, both foliose, one ranging in color from yellow to nearly orange, the other much less prolific variety a greenish gray. The lichens also offered testimony to the purity of the environment from which they had been taken. Pollution is one of the few conditions they cannot tolerate. Farm groves and the industrial sections of cities are not good places to hunt for them.

Cattail seeds had become snared in the tangled branches of the lichens. The seeds had burst from their cigarlike moorings on stems now anchored in ice, and at every hint of a breeze they went sailing through the air by the thousands of thousands. A thousand of the incredibly delicate parachutes would not make a mass in the palm of one's hand dense enough to give an impression of weight. Most of them would come, like the seeds of this piece of bark, to nothing, to places high and dry and far even from potential fruition. Some of them would land in places where they would lie dormant for many years, until there would be the one lingering puddle of water of the quarter-century. Then they would spring abundantly up and make of the place an instant marsh, as if marshes leaked forth somehow full-grown from invisible fissures in the earth.

There was another seed on the bit of bark, the much heavier, three-cornered pod of the water-plaintain fruit. The water-plaintain, a plant of shallow, mud-bottomed waters, is given to threes: its stems are tri-angular; its flower stalks often grow in whorls of three; its fruits have three sepals; it grows to three or three-and-something feet. The pod was stuck to a strand of the spider's web, now collapsed, and near it was a long, black hair, perhaps the hair of the creature that had carried it away from its watery birthplace. Certainly, the seed could not have arrived on its own. It was made to float, not to fly. I could not name the owner of the black hair.

There was also the dried leaf of a wild plum. It was caught in another strand of the spider's webbing, which ran everywhere across the
scrap of bark. The plum and the cottonwood grew in happy associa-
tion with one another. The plum was made to be low and rambling.
It did not aspire to heights. It grew in upon itself. The cottonwood
was just the opposite. It grew at a frenzied pace, three or four feet a
year when it received enough water. It cast off branches right and left,
sloughed off its bark, regularly conceded whole sections of its trunk
to wind and ice, transpired water as if there was no end to it when it
was available, held on grandly as if it had, really, no appetite at all for
water in times of drought.

So the canopy of the plum hunched low to the earth and was impenetrable to all but the smallest creatures, and the canopy of the
cottonwood reached as extravagantly as it could for the ultimate
heights, inviting the company of hawks and owls. There was space
and water enough for the two kinds of trees, so different in character,
to spread out roots together in the same soil. In doing so, they demonstrated one of the principles upon which the prairie was made, the
principle of diversity. It is in the alliance of differences that the prairie
finds its vigor; it fashions its resilience and stability in the clash of
countervailing strengths and weaknesses.

In this, the natural order stands at direct odds with the kind of
order we ourselves impose. The nature of our own vision consists in
seeing things, as in the cornfield that comes down to the edge of the
community of cottonwoods and plums, in categories. In the natural
order, the tendency is toward interdependence, whereas in the human
imagination, it is toward distinctions.

I turned over my scrap of bark and gave attention to its interior
surface. A number of creatures that had been dormant in the frigid
winter air bestirred themselves. I found a little hopper and a dozen
pale and immature spiders. (Most of the spiders would be gone in another day. There was little sustenance in my study for a gathering of
spiders.) I also uncovered a stone fly that had been hibernating in the
open spring at the foot of the tree from which the bark had come. And
one or two other flying creatures escaped, too small and too quick for
me to catch.

There were other evidences of insect life: the outer wings of a ladybug and of another beetle; a bit of the nest of a mud dauber wasp; the egg sacks of two species of spiders, one of them containing the remains of sixty-seven hatched eggs; the ceilings of a series of carpenter ant chambers; two or three other deposits of eggs which I could not name; the scattered remnants of chitin from other sources.

I might have attempted a long list of the transient visitors to this bit of bark, this inconsequential speck in the wide world of the prairies. Over the six or seven decades of the existence of this piece of bark, there would have been unnumbered thousands of visitors representing, certainly, hundreds of species of living things.

I might have repaired to a microscope for a look at the creatures that live out their lives beyond range of the naked human eye. There must have been thousands of them on this piece of bark, thousands whose names I could not tell, whose lives I could not recount, whose place in the scheme of things I did not know and could not guess. It frustrated me that I could attach names to so few of the things I saw.

A name is the first gift we give a child. Long before the baby has come, almost from the day they are certain there has been a conception, human parents begin to deliberate over the choosing of a name. It should be a name that sounds good. It must not be a name attached to a person either parent dislikes. If the name has some historical resonance, all the better; if it continues a line of names in the family, if it immortalizes a hero of the culture, or if it is a name that also describes one of the saints, let it be considered. The name will be pretty or plain; it will be unusual or ordinary; it will suggest creed and nationality and race; it will be the same as papa's, or it will be notably unlike papa's; it will be modest or assuming; it will be solemn or lighthearted; it will be a name like Ricky, forever youthful, or it will be a name like Elizabeth, forever grown-up; it will be reassuring, or it will be intimidating; it will be hard to make into a nickname, or it will be made to be amended. In the gift of a name, a parent bequeaths to a child an identity, a set of values, a constant reminder of particular hopes and dreams. It is a gift the child will spend a whole lifetime either accepting or rejecting.

I cannot see that there is anything of substance in a name itself, however substantial it might eventually come to be. A name is not an object of substance, like a beam of light or the bud of a cottonwood or the sawing of a cricket. What makes it real is the set of associations it is forever bringing into the minds of those who hear or pronounce it. These mental ascriptions are the product of chemical and electrical impulses, and these impulses have substance; they are momentary manifestations of the person named inside the mind of the person doing the naming. To name a thing is, in some literal sense, to take possession of it.

I wanted to name all the strange creatures that had taken up habitation in the bit of bark that rested upon my study table because I wanted to have possession of them. I cannot think of any other way in which I might have come into acquaintance with, say, the spider fetus hanging in a sac from the lower left corner of the interior surface of my fragment of dead cottonwood. The only alternative was the one I was now confronted with: by not knowing the name of the thing, I was rendered mute before it—unable to make any concrete observation about it, even about its appearance or manner; unable to say for certain anything about the creature's habits or its companions or its style of living. Without its name, this creature rested before me as mysterious as a black hole in space or the cuneiform writings of the Mayans or the events to come in the second after next.

To be nameless is to be silent, and to be silent is to be estranged from the human mind. So this piece of bark resting upon my study table was to say nothing after all. It was to remain a mystery to me in the end, like all the rest of the natural world. There might be wondrous abundance here. There might be manifest evidence in it of the variousness of life. But as long as it had no name, it had nothing to say, no instruction to impart. It could not be reconstructed, made real in the mind.

It was little enough to come alive in the human mind in any case. Every day, the sun showers down 120 tons of energy upon the earth. The leaves of this cottonwood with the leaves of all the other plants in the world manage to capture some few thousand pounds of this energy each day and convert it to sugar. Eventually, some percentage of this frozen energy becomes the property of humans and of the portion they use; something amounting to no more than a few billionths of a gram of this energy goes in any one day to power all the thoughts in all the minds of all the people upon earth. And the sun is one insignificant star among a hundred billion stars in one galaxy among a hundred billion galaxies in the universe.

8

One fundamental fact of life on the wild prairies is danger. I am reminded of this nearly every winter morning when I come out of my secure house in my safe little prairie town and walk around a placid lake toward the soothing security of my warm and inviolate office. Along the route I take most mornings, a little drainage ditch runs into the lake, and beyond its bank stands a utility shed that has been obscured by a planting of pine trees. These pines make a splendid snow fence in winter and a fine hiding place in summer. A thicket of young willows also grows between the pines and the water in the ditch.

The place is home for two or three of the town's rabbits. They live in dens in the snowbanks there in the wintertime. The entrances to these dens are not obvious, and the rabbits keep out of sight during the day. Most people who pass are unaware of their existence.

I make my own passage in the very early morning. In the wintertime, it is hours before the break of dawn. Often at that time of day, the rabbits feed under the light of a streetlamp upon the branches of the young willows. Sometimes I pause while I am still a little way off and watch them, but however long I wait, I never see one of them resume business as normal. Upon the first warning of my presence, they freeze in their tracks and stay frozen until I either pass by or come so close that they are compelled to dart for safety. I have never happened upon a cottontail unawares. The rabbit has always, no matter where it was or what it had been doing, seen me first and taken some defensive posture.

To be a cottontail is to be forever on the defensive. Danger flies everywhere through the air and crawls or runs everywhere upon the earth. The rabbit is equally vulnerable to night predators and to day predators. It has resorted in self-defense to living out its active life in the brief interlude between darkness and daylight.

There are few creatures in the prairie world that do not also live with the perpetual possibility of violence. To die that others might live is the natural way. Only the largest of predators can expect to reach the biological limits of their lives subject merely to the hazards of weather, of accident, of disease, of some genetic flaw. For the rest, the condition of life is to be hunted.

I was walking across the Cayler Prairie one early February evening when it seemed to me that winter is not so much the season of dormancy as the season of truce.

The Cayler is an unusually large prairie remnant for cornbelt country, 160 acres, and it is unusual too because it has been under good management for half a century. It lies at the center of a section of land in a terminal moraine in northwest Iowa; it is, therefore, gently rolling. Because of its size and of its location in the section and of its topography, it is one of the few places in my part of the world where one can get out of sight of the artifacts of civilization and begin to see the tallgrass prairie landscape as it might have been a couple of centuries ago.

The Cayler does not abut, as so many remnants do, an abandoned farm grove or the shore of a prairie lake or the edge of a substantial wetland. It is the prairie our ancestors knew when they settled here: high, dry, wind-swept. There is no place to hide on the Cayler. This was the feature of the prairie landscape that overwhelmed so many pioneers, the realization that it was so exposed, so naked. There was something relentless about the scale of it.

One can feel that relentlessness even now on the Cayler, especially as twilight falls over it on a silent and icy day in February. I made my way across it on foot. It was heavy going. The snow was crusted and would support the weight of a human where it was hard-packed. But the substrate of this snow was the dense prairie foliage, which had made room for air pockets in many places in the drifts. Every second or third step was above one of those pockets, into which I sank to a depth of two or three feet. The snow was evenly distributed. It was no easier going on the swells than in the swales.

I circled for a couple of hours through the prairie remnant. I went even more slowly than the snow required me to go. I carried a pair of binoculars. I watched the skies. I kept my eyes sharp for any sign of life on the surface of the snow or beneath it. Once or twice I thought I had seen something, but it always turned out to be the inflorescence of some prairie plant bent at a deceptive angle. I searched the tops of the hills. I circled their slopes. I walked the shallow valleys. I hunted through the thicket of willows, the little pothole in the southwestern corner of the prairie, the stand of wolf berries opposite the hilltop where the prairie smoke is so spectacular in the spring. I looked into the clumps of golden-rod, into the tufts of the bluestems, into the places where the cordgrass had been bent over and frozen into genuflection in the rough ice.

In one or two places I saw the hard droppings of cottontails. (They themselves had consumed the softer wastes.) Atop a couple of apparently vacant muskrat houses in the tiny pothole, a few tracks showed, old and obscured. Another set of tracks led out of the pothole and toward the township road that passed along the western edge of the prairie. But I could find no fresh sign of active life anywhere on that high and exposed remnant of lost world: no bird in the sky, no new track underfoot, no stray tuft of hair or feather in the grass to give some sign of life on earth or above it.

With one exception. Elaborate chambers were tunneled in the thick prairie sod, each of them with an exit through the snow to the featureless plain above. These exits tended to be hidden in bunches of grass, but they could not be altogether obscured. The tunnels were the passageways and dwelling places of the resident mice and voles and shrews, which either alternated between hibernation and feeding or remained active throughout the winter. They were the seed-eating rodents. They would be subsisting now mainly on the stores they had put away before snowfall, although when these supplies ran low, some sustenance was still to be had from the roots and stems that were exposed along the corridors of their hidden houses.

In spring, in summer, in fall, the rodents, like the rabbits, had to be constantly on guard. Every creature, from one of its larger relatives on up the food chain to the foxes and coyotes and wolves and including all the birds of prey, might find a rodent to be a suitable meal.

Many of the predators were still alive in winter. They had no subterranean dens in which to hide. Foxes and coyotes were still on the prowl. Owls still cruised the skies. There were still crows. Weasels were about. But the odds in early and midwinter eased a bit for once in favor of the rodent prey. The numbers of active predators were down; it was much more difficult for them to move across the landscape now; the rodents had little reason to stray beyond their chambers into danger; even when they had been located, it was difficult enough for a predator to get at them through the snow.

So it was a time when the ceaseless killing tempered, if not the dying; when even a little meadow mouse might get a brief and uncertain taste of security; when there was, if ever, peace and goodwill on earth.

The supremacy of the rodents on that winter day made their fecundity apparent. Fecundity is the strategy of nature against the harshness of life. The point is not the survival of the individual. Individuals are never destined to survive for very long. Nor is the survival of the species the point. Species come and go. The point is the survival of life itself.

Our own particular fecundity, the fecundity of the mind, has altered the long-range odds against the survival of life, at least here on this planet in this corner of the universe. And what of the time, perhaps four and a half million years from now, when our star has exhausted itself? What then?

We are all like the observer in the Wallace Stevens poem who

    . . . listens in the snow,
    And nothing himself, beholds

Nothing that is not there and nothing that is.
We are the snow men.

9

Silver Lake, late afternoon. Everything was gray: the sky; the ice; the snow, both the old and the freshly fallen; the water running from the spring into the lake; the bent cattail reeds in the shallows of the lake; the thicket of willows between the lake and the fen; the tall stalks of *Phragmites* growing upon the fen; the cottonwoods on the knoll beyond it; the tracks of rabbits and partridges in the wild plum thicket; the sound of the north wind, of the trickle of springwater, of one cattail reed rubbing against another. Everything was gray, more the color of pewter than of silver, although it must have been in memory of such a day that Silver Lake was named.

The wind was neither strong, nor bitter, although it was blowing out of the north. The snowfall was light. It was like a Thanksgiving snow, crystals so big you could see them individually as they came down. The wind was driving them at an angle as long and low as the angle of the winter sun.

I had come to the lake because I had been writing about it for days, and the more I wrote about it, the less I could remember of it. To write about something is to take leave of it. I needed to find my sense of the lake again. So I went down to the waters of one of the springs that feeds it, expecting to find some sign of fresh life to color over my own grayness. As I was standing there, the bank of snow gave way, and I was plunged in. It was not the thing I had imagined I might find.

I went back to the car for a snowmobile suit to cover my sodden legs and then took a stand on higher ground to await some development, I knew not what. I don't suppose, thinking back on it, that anything ever did develop. There was no event, in any case. Nothing of a material sort. No news.

What happened was that everything already there grew somehow both more intense and more abstract. Standing there, I fell into a kind of reverie. I do not know how to tell of this, although I have had the experience before in the wintertime when the snow was falling. Three of my earliest and most vivid memories have to do with revelations in the falling snow.

I remember riding to town in a storm and taking notice for the first time of the snow running in streams across the highway and having a vision of it as somehow animate. I saw myself being chased by the snow as by a beast. It had stuck in my head that we were going to a store called Monkey Wards, I can't remember why, and when we got there it turned out, to my bitter disappointment, that there were no monkeys. I thought at first that if I could only see up over the counters, I might find them. But when we were on our way home again, I saw that the snow was still running after us, and I believed that it had seized the monkeys and that it might at any moment snatch us too.

I was quite a bit older, almost four, when my grandfather died. I remember sitting in the parlor of his house in the presence of his corpse and of being nauseated by the scent of flowers and of body perfume. We waited a very long time in that parlor, and the odors of the place grew as we sat there, waiting, I suppose, for condolences to be said. The room grew cloyingly hot. There was a tropical steaminess about it. But when we went out to bury my grandfather, we encountered a bitter wind, and the snow was running again. For a long time after that, I smelled the odor of death in the snow winds.

Very much later, when I was ten or twelve, I walked out one violent winter day into a ground blizzard. I was afraid of it, but I was also curious, and what I found altogether astonished me. I couldn't see ten feet in any direction in the swirling of the snow, and I couldn't hear anything except the roaring of the wind. The experience, I would learn a couple of decades later, was like walking through a cloud. There was something quite tranquil, something strangely intimate, about coming into a landscape altogether without recognizable features. It ceased to be frightening to me then, and I have not been frightened, against all reason, by any blizzard since. Above the clouds of snow, the sun was shining, and its light was refracted in the crystals of snow into all the colors of the rainbow, but delicately, like the colors of wild flowers. What I found in the eye of that blizzard was a vision of flowers.

At Silver Lake, the north wind blew, the big flakes of snow came down like airplanes landing, the light of the sun receded, and a kind of distillation began to occur. The wind, which had seemed gentle, began to moan, or perhaps to sigh, an involuntary expression of loneliness. The cold settled as a dull and not at all unpleasant ache in my bones. The gray color of everything became less blue and more gray.

Perhaps I was experiencing a magnification rather than a distillation. The sensations that came into my eyes and ears began to break apart like the grains of color in a photographic negative magnified too many times. A cattail reed twenty yards away slapped in a sudden gust of wind, and I was startled by the gigantic sound of it.

I felt myself slipping away into a blueness of my own. My sense of my size in relation to the landscape diminished. The hills beyond the lake seemed to recede; its opposite shore seemed to pull away; it got harder and harder to make out the waving line of the *Phragmites* on the fen that rose between the lake and the hills. What had seemed a unity of land and sky and water now began to disintegrate. The landscape seemed increasingly to be a succession of lines—the line of hills, the line of trees, the line of reeds, the line of cattails, the line of water— and less and less did there seem to be any communication among them. I increasingly made my own distinct and disparate mark on the landscape.

I understood how this sensation, running on until the days stretched into weeks and the weeks into months, could drive a person mad. In fact, it did. Not far from this place, there was a barn where, it is said, in a single winter three unrelated pioneers retreated, one after the other, to hang themselves.

And then in the sky overhead, another line appeared, a high-flying wedge of snow geese heading north at midwinter. They must have been moving at forty miles per hour. Their high-spirited honking drifted down to earth. They flew on another mile and suddenly descended to earth in a squabble of confusion. There was silence again. But the fact of the wind and the cold had somehow been taken away.

10

It was not yet March, and the fen at the edge of Silver Lake was still frozen, but the warm air and the brilliant rays of the sun and the absence of motion gave the impression of a lazy Sunday afternoon in midsummer.

It was like waking up from a nap after lunch and feeling a lingering grogginess and finding a ring of sweat around your neck at the collar-line and being half-bored and half-charmed. The season was like that, caught in a dreamy limbo between waking and sleeping.

In the plum thicket and in the tangled web of cattail reeds at the edge of the lake, there were congregations of tree sparrows. The sparrows flitted here and there and called out now and then, lending little color but some dance and song to the otherwise dormant stage.

The ice among the cattails was already showing the pockmarks of age. Beneath it in one or two places, little brooks of meltwater bubbled and gurgled.

Into this somnolent landscape burst suddenly a bee, a very loud and very busy bee. It flew several feet above the icy surface of the marsh quickly and in a straight line away from the willows along the lakeshore. Perhaps it was on its way back to its nest.

The bee announced the life that, though silent and unseen, was already stirring on the edges of the still-firm bog along Silver Lake. The buzzing of the bee said that the frost was out at the edge of the marsh, that the sap was flowing in the veins of the willows, that the trees had already begun to produce pollen. It was the pollen in the willows that the bee had gone out to collect.

There had been other signs of the turn in the seasons: the faint odor of skunk in the air, the carcasses of two skunks along the road on the way to the fen. The slow-moving skunks, on the prowl for mates now, were vulnerable to the hazards of traffic. And the stench of the cattail marsh was already in the air, the fetid evidence of the billions of microbes at work in the fecund litter of the marsh floor. It was a smell like the aroma of the skunk; overpoweringly sweet, penetrating and impossible to get rid of.

When the bee had disappeared, a new and deathly silence fell upon the brilliantly lit earth.

There seemed not to be another living thing in all the world. There was something of bliss in this stillness, and something ominous in it too. It was the kind of stillness that beckons us to turn inward, toward the beginnings of our existence.

And then in the distance could be heard the sound of a flock of blackbirds arriving, a rustling sound like the wind in the leaves of the cottonwood. The next night, the thunder cracked and the first rain of spring fell.

Spring

1

On the day after the ice went out, the seasons passed tumultuously across the prairies in a twenty-four hour retrospective, like the scenes of life in a dying person's eyes.

The day was gray-brown, the color of marsh mud. When it dawned, a great cloud of gulls hovered over the lake, circling and diving and shrieking. Above them ducks quacked as they sped north. And above them were geese, some high enough to be out of sight but not out of sound.

Other birds of the day seemed earthbound by comparison: the robins and wrens, the crows and blackbirds, the sparrows and chickadees, the flickers and bluejays, the tree birds, the birds of the soil, singing every one. The birds seemed as numerous as the stars. They were bursting upon the morning sky like fireworks and falling to the far ends of the earth.

The air was warm and heavy with moisture. By noon, it was shirtsleeve weather. The wind carried the smell of summer, of things rotting. It was the kind of weather that beckons you out-of-doors and then makes you feel too heavy for activity.

By midmorning, great black stormclouds had arisen in the west. The thunder in them rumbled. It looked and sounded deceptively like the advent of an August storm.

In another hour, thick drops of rain began to fall. They coated everything with a sheen that glistened in the yellow light: the trunks of trees, the pavement, the bare earth, the mats of dead leaves, the furled leaves of emerging tulips, the roofs of houses, the olive needles of pine trees—everything gleamed in the cleansing and greening wash of spring.

In yet another hour, the winds quickened and began to howl around the corners of houses and in the gyrating branches of the bare wet trees. The raindrops turned to ice, fell as stinging arrows of sleet, as little pellets of hail. The ice turned to snow, and the white pall of winter fell over the landscape: over the nests of spiders, over the yellowing crowns of the domestic grasses, over the uncovered flower beds, over the first forgotten tricycles of the season.

Long after the snow ceased to fall, the winds howled on. Dawn came, and still they blew, whipping up the thin cover of snow into a parody of a blizzard, picking up the water on the surface of the lake, gathering it into sheets and sending it spraying over the ducks that had come down out of the storm and were riding it out along the southwestern shore of the lake. Banks rose there and supported thick-trunked willow trees that took the brunt of the weather.

The storm would not be long in passing. Soon there would be calm again and warmer weather and gentler rains and the inevitable progress toward new life.

It was always so, that there should be a struggle, the tumult before the calm, that life should be freshly captured by each new generation and not simply handed down like the baby's old clothes.

2

Mid-March. The sap was running again in the trees. At the sources of the springs, the cattails were sprouting again. In the brown under-thicket of the meadows, the leaves of the wild strawberries made a brilliant show of green on St. Patrick's day. The pocket gophers were bringing fresh dirt up from their burrows to the surface of the earth. Everywhere it was beginning to be spring.

The person who walked to work in the dark and went home again in the dark through the long winter now enjoyed the breaking of the light at both ends of the day. It brightened the spirits. It was energizing. It was exhausting. People humped along with watery eyes and swollen sinuses. They complained of feeling tired for no good reason. In churches, people were singing the dirges of Lent.

But there were no dirges in the wetlands. There the siren song of official spring could be heard at every hand: the glorious trumpeting of the geese. The geese on the potholes trumpeted to the geese flying in wedges overhead, and the geese overhead trumpeted to the geese feeding in the cornfields, and the geese in the cornfields trumpeted to the wide world.

What is it in the call of a goose that is so magical? Is it the volume of it, so deliciously brazen after the months of wintery silence? Is it the appealingly adolescent quality of it, the way it starts in a resonant baritone and suddenly tumbles out of control into a high squeak, that delirious, schoolchildish sound? Is it the humor of it after a season of seriousness and solitude, the improbability of such an uninhibited call gushing forth from a creature so elegant in flight, so formal in adornment? Aldo Leopold has it right: the call speaks to us of the conviction that propels a goose forward into the feckless northland spring.

"A cardinal, whistling spring to a thaw but later finding himself mistaken, can retrieve his error by resuming his winter silence," Leopold wrote in A Sand County Almanac. "A chipmunk, emerging for a sunbath but finding a blizzard, has only to go back to bed. But a migrating goose, staking two hundred miles of flight on the chance of finding a hole in the lake, has no easy chance for retreat. His arrival carries the conviction of a prophet who has burned his bridges."

On a marsh near Indian Lake, a pair of geese passed overhead and came to rest on top of a muskrat lodge. A pair of geese nested in the same place last year. Were they the same geese? Perhaps. Geese are given to family life.

They brought to us a cosmopolitan presence, some connection with the tundras of Hudson's Bay and the salty waters of the Gulf of Mexico. They made us an international port of call.

Leopold again:

> It is an irony of history that the great powers should have discovered the unity of nations at Cairo in 1943. The geese of the world have had that notion for a longer time, and each March they stake their lives on its essential truth.

In the beginning there was only the unity of the Ice Sheet. Then followed the unity of the March thaw, and the northward hegira of the international geese. Every March since the Pleistocene, the geese have honked unity from China Sea to Siberian Steppe, from Euphrates to Volga, from Nine to Murmansk, from Lincolnshire to Spitsbergen. Every March since the Pleistocene, the geese have honked unity from Currituck to Labrador, Matamuskeet to Ungava, Horseshoe Lake to Hudson's Bay. Avery Island to Baffin Land, Panhandle to McKenzie, Sacramento to Yukon.

By this international commerce of geese, the waste corn of Illinois is carried through the clouds of the Artic tundras, there to combine with the waste sunlight of a nightless June to grow goslings for all lands between. And in this annual barter of food for light, and winter warmth for summer solitude, the whole continent receives as net profit a wild poem dropped from murky skies upon the muds of March.

A late storm rolled in, taking a heavy toll of birds. For days afterward the snow lingered, snuggled against the green furls of the spring-flowering bulbs, covering the debris the melt had revealed. Open water still lapped against the brown stems of the reeds in the ponds. Beneath the snow, the ground had thawed, but the landscape looked wintry, and its appearance made it feel like winter. Then as suddenly as the storm had come, the thaw returned, and this time it was final.

A thunderstorm arrived one night and laid waste to the sleeping chambers of the earthworms, caving some in, flooding others. By the scores of thousands, the worms worked their way up to the surface of the earth. There they were snatched up in great numbers by the migrating birds and eaten.

In the marshes, the snails had been at last set free from their prisons of ice. Some of them were dead and sank to the bottom of the marshes. Others swam free and set about their business of foraging.

Spring peepers made their way out of the bottom mud and took up a noisy chorus.

The white pelicans swept through, making feasts of the fish on the lakes. In the days before settlement, some of them would have stayed and nested on Heron Lake and on other bodies of water nearby, but now they honored us merely by pausing in our midst.

The bees were out of their hives; the first hatch of mosquitoes had become pests; and the harvester ants were out in swarms, tending to such repairs of their elaborate mound-villages as the heavings of the frost and the running of the meltwaters had made necessary.

In the high places, the anemones were up, and in the low places and along the banks of the prairie creeks, the stinging nettles were making a show of lacy greenery.

Sounds had come back into the landscape. The noises of birds, of insects, of frogs had made the still barren surfaces of things seem alive and vibrant. One heard the winds and the rains of spring, the greening and drying forces of a vast solar energy.

On the dry southeastern faces of the prairie hills, the first native flowers of the spring, the pasqueflowers, were in bloom again. Pasqueflowers, like so many early-season flowers, are colored in the palest of pastels, the better to attract notice among the weathered and lifeless browns of spring.

Their petals are formed in a wide, deep saucer an inch deep and an inch and a half across. The petals make the shape of a solar dish collector, and in fact they function as one. On a sunny day in early spring, the temperature inside a pasqueflower might be as much as 18° F higher than the temperature of the air around it. The stamens and carpels in the center of the pasqueflowers are covered with many hairs, which serve as temporary storage bins for the heat the petals collect.

The pasque blossoms rise on stems that thrust themselves above the litter of the grassland floor and directly into the sunlight. The stems are flexible and capable of wide-ranging rotation, so that the collector dish can always be positioned at an advantageous angle to the sun.

At night or when the skies are cloudy, the petals close, shutting in the precious heat that has been trapped in happier lights.

The flowers attract the few passing insects, which linger in their warmth. They put up with the meager supply of nectar that the pasque-flowers hold in store. The pasqueflowers get pollinated, and the insects get warm, sometimes even to the extent of spending the night inside the closed petals and the flowers. The whole exchange costs almost nothing, least of all to the pasqueflowers.

Pasqueflowers bloom at an inhospitable time in a quirky season. They carry the impression of wit and grace. If a pasqueflower were a person, one would want to have it home to dinner at the first opportunity. Surely, that would be the occasion for much laughter and bright conversation.

3

By the second week in April, the pasqueflowers on the south-facing prairie slopes had faded and fallen away, and their still-fuzzy leaves had begun to open. On the southwest-facing slopes, however, the flowers were just beginning to show. They would be at their best by Easter. The lead plants were growing, and the violets were making a splash of green here and there.

But the prairie, despite the early coming of spring, was still mainly clothed in the brown and severe dress of winter. The prairie is late-sleeping and late-blooming. The lushest time of the year on the prairie, the time when it displays its brightest colors, is autumn.

It was one of the things that made the prairie vulnerable to the weeds the settlers brought with them when they turned the centuries-old sod into fields of wheat and corn. The plants imported from Europe were for the most part early risers. When the protective cover of the sod had been broken, the newcomers were always able to win the race to claim the barren earth.

On the remnants of the virgin ground, the shrews and the moles had by now delivered their young; the ground squirrels were about to; and the geese had gone off to nest. Every pothole and marsh temporarily housed a noisy flock of feeding ducks. Every telephone wire seemed to support a western meadowlark singing its song. The juncos, the chickadees, and the nuthatches had left the backyard feeders and headed elsewhere. If the prairie was still brown, the movement toward high spring was inescapably under way.

4

In the fleeting days of April, in the first days of May:

The purple martins returned.

The butterflies emerged.

The frogs began to sing again in the dusk of evening at the waterholes.

The plums burst into fragrant blossom.

The nests of robins were filled with bright blue eggs.

The young cottontail rabbits made quivering forays from home and scampered back into hiding at the slightest sign of danger.

The bumblebees, the independent members of a gregarious family, settled their huge gilded bodies onto delicate flowers.

Violets and dandelions bloomed by the millions.

The prairie grasses began to awaken.

A visitor walking the edge of a prairie lake at dawn in these days was heralded along the way by the quacking of retreating ducks.

And these days brought the squalls and great winds of springtime. The winds seemed to follow the birds up from the south. They were like the furies in the ancient plays, like choruses of monsters come to hurl a final gale of insults at retreated winter before the shimmering and indolent days of summer. I set foot one late April afternoon in one of these torrents of wind. It was like a dream.

The sound of the wind overrode all other sounds. Birds disappeared. People disappeared. Automobile traffic disappeared. The wind wrapped around me like a skin.

The fine residue of topsoil in the air settled in my teeth and made a grinding grit at the nape of my neck. The dust settled in my eyes. They burned and watered. I narrowed them to slits and scowled.

I was carrying my mail. The wind whipped and tugged at it and tore it to shreds. The friction of the wind against my face began to burn the skin on my cheeks. I took on a blush.

The wind did not come at me in one steady blast. It was coquettish, but too rough to be really playful. It tossed me here and there, forward and back, rendered me as helpless as the treetops that also bowed and writhed before the wind.

On another day in early May, I went driving in a spring wind. My car bucked. The wind carried such a heavy load of earth that at times it was difficult to see through it to the center stripe on the highway. The earth filtered through the cracks of the car windows and settled in the furrows of my brow.

After such winds, I embraced the quiet of a house well-sheltered. In the peace of it, I tried to imagine how life must have been in the prairie days before sturdy houses and the shelter of full-grown trees, how desperately people must sometimes have yearned to be free of the winds, how reverently they came to worship and fear the winds that brought both feast and famine.

They are, I acknowledged, one of the requisite rigors of the prairie world. They both test and improve the character of its inhabitants. But I had just come in out of a spring wind. I was content for the moment to be neither tested nor improved.

There is a paradox in the havoc that the winds make upon the prairie: there would not be prairies without them. Actually, it is difficult to say what did make the prairies. They advanced and retreated in episodes stretching over millennia. When white people arrived to settle the country where I live, the prairies were in a period of retreat. I do not have to look very far back in history to find the time when the lands I have grown accustomed to thinking of as naturally prairie were, in fact, forests. Pollen samples from sediment cores taken in Lake Okoboji show my place was a spruce forest only 10,000 years ago. The deepest sediments in the core bear signs of musk oxen. The subarctic forest was wiped out by a glacier. Grasslands grew up in its place, but perhaps without the interruption of agriculture there would have been forest again. Whatever complex set of events made conditions favorable for prairie, the winds were prominent among them.

Before the ice, perhaps 65 million years ago at the end of the

Cretaceous period, a geological riot, known as the Laramie Revolution, gave us the spectacular mountains of the West, the Rockies, the Sierra Madres, the Sierra Nevadas.

It was in the rain shadow of these mountains, perhaps 25 million years ago, that the grasslands of the central plains began to emerge. The air masses that reached the central plains still came from the Pacific, but by the time they got there, they had already been interrupted by three ranges of mountains, each extracting its own bit of the water vapor they were carrying. By the time the winds reached the plains they were nearly dry. Still they blew, speeding the transpiration of water from the plants, and drying out the highly permeable glacial soils that covered 70 percent of the land that would become the domain of the grasses. In the long shadow of the mountains, the climate became inhospitable to trees.

The great central grasslands took their present shape during the final ice age, which lasted 100,000 years during the Pleistocene era, and which made of the Upper Mississippi Valley a vast arctic waste. When the ice retreated, its water running away in great glacial rivers to the sea, a fine, mineral-rich till remained. It was exposed to the winds, which were even then prevailingly westerlies. These made of the powdered rock dust storms, which raged ceaselessly, eventually drifting what are now called loess soils across large stretches of the ice-flattened lands that were to become the prairies.

Four periods of glaciation occurred on the northern plains, the last of them still lingering in northern Minnesota scarcely 9,000 years ago. And there were fluctuations in climate. Now it was warmer; now it was colder; now there was drought; now the rainfall was heavier than usual. The forests advanced in warmer, wetter periods; they retreated in colder, drier times. But after the great mountain ranges of the West had risen, there was always a place on the plains where the critical ratio of precipitation to evaporation tilted in favor of the grasses. Grasses are wonderfully well suited to the capricious prairie winds.

For one thing, they grow from the roots up. A grass seedling shows only modest top growth for the first three or four years of its life. It spends much of its energy in building a dense underground support system. Its roots grow deep enough to take advantage of subsoil stores of water in times of drought, and they grow wide enough to catch the nutriment and moisture in the upper levels of the soil in times of normal rainfall. The grasses make a forest that grows underground instead of aboveground, and an incredible thicket it is. A square meter of prairie sod might contain twenty-five miles of roots.

The sod is a mighty armament against the vagaries of the weather. When the winds blow, it holds the movable soils firmly in place. When rains fall, it prevents the soils from washing away. The sod also sponges up the precious rainfall and releases it into the earth slowly so that as it percolates down, it becomes rich with the minerals the soil gives up. The sod acts as a cover to retard evaporation in the summer heat, and it insulates the life below its surface during the long winter freeze. It is a shield against the bruising hooves of the antelope and bison and elk. It is home to most of the creatures that have come to live upon the prairies; it made the raw material for the first homes of the white people.

When grass has rooted itself, it sends up its top growth, which might be a few inches high on the arid high plains or eight or nine feet high on the moistest prairies of the east. The stem of a grass is a hollow, silica-reinforced tube sturdied at regular intervals by thickened nodes. Its construction makes it incredibly strong—no stronger design exists in nature—but also quite flexible. It is made to take the steady beating of the winds.

Its leaves are long and narrow. It is possible to pack a great many of them into a small area. A stand of grass presents a far greater proportion of leaf surface to the sun than does an equivalent growth of trees. At the same time, these narrow leaves present a limited profile to the drying winds. When the sun is at its most brutal in mid-August, the grass leaves are made to curl in upon themselves, to hide their stoma from the devastating heat. The leaves are arranged in sheaves around the grass stems. When it rains, the arrangement breaks the fall of the water and channels it in streams down the stems to the central core of roots.

The dense sod and the happy arrangement of leaves have a dramatic effect on the climate at ground level, where the life of the prairie, given the limited reach of its canopy, is necessarily heavily concentrated. In a stand of native grasses, the temperature may be as much as 10 percent higher than at soil level in an adjacent field of corn.

The grasses, for the most part, have modest flowers. Although many of these are quite beautiful under the magnification of a hand lens, they are so unassuming in general that most people are never aware of them. The grasses do not need showy flowers to attract pollinating insects. They depend upon the winds for pollination, just as they depend upon the winds to scatter their seeds.

The grasses have several strategies for reproduction: they can extend their territory by seeds, which can remain viable for decades after they are produced; they regenerate themselves on shoots growing up from old roots; they send out runners on the surface of the soil to establish new plants.

Because it grows from its base rather than from its tip, a grass is made to withstand abuse. Break it off in the wind, cut it, trample it, mangle it to shreds in a hailstorm, pull it up—do what you might, in a week or two, a grass will be back as green and healthy as ever.

On the bare quartzite rocks atop the Blue Mounds, in the soggy alkaline seepages of the Silver Lake Fen, in the sand hills of western Nebraska, on the exposed knolls of gravel in the glacial moraines, wherever life is thin and stunted, there one can always find a species of grass, and not just one spear of it but a whole colony. Grass is by its nature a colonizer. It is the army that has always marched at the forefront of advanced life, even as it embraced, beginning 25 million years ago, the wide spaces of the American plains, where the winds blew, and tamed them into the wonder that now feeds the world.

5

In the aftermath of its spring burning, the Compass Prairie looked as pockmarked and burrowed and mounded, as battered and scarred as the poor moon itself. To walk across it now was to see the scattered bones of the creatures that had recently given their lives on it, and to feel the thick carpet of sod that made a mantle over the precious soil.

To a great extent, life on the prairie is lived in underground burrows of one kind or another. Badger holes, ground squirrel holes, pocket gopher holes, the holes of mice and moles, the excavations of ants, at marsh level the burrows of crayfish and the channels made by muskrats, each with its mound of displaced earth, came into view on the ashen landscape that the fire had exposed. It was apparent that the digging of these creatures subjected the prairie to something like a regular, collective plowing. There were also the heavings and grindings of the freezes and thaws, the vast workings of the earthworms, and the tunnelings of insects. Together they worked to bring up trace elements from the subsoil to the growing zones of the earth, to keep the soil soft and pliable and receptive to the fall of the rains, and to make beds suitable for the growth of new seeds. It is one of many strategies for regeneration that has sustained the prairie.

Fire is another of them. Fire is the great prairie emancipator. Where the litter of dead plant matter has accumulated to oppressive depth, fire brings the freedom of air and light. The black rubble blots the warm rays of the spring sun, speeding the warming of the springtime earth. Plant growth will come sooner and will be more vigorous where there has been fire.

As plants grow and die and become part of the litter of the prairie floor, they absorb quantities of nutrients from the earth. Fire liberates these nutrients too, making the potash and phosphorus and some of the trace minerals available to be leached back into the earth again. The nitrogen in the plant material goes up with the smoke into the air. It comes down again in the form of rain. The burned-over prairie will be ready to capture it. Fire seems to stimulate the growth of some legumes, leadplant among them. Legumes have the ability, in cooperation with certain bacteria, to recapture nitrogen from the dissolved substances in the water they take up through their roots.

Where trees and grasses have battled for supremacy, fire has been a critical influence. When fires prevailed, grasses extended their dominion. When they did not, trees took root. Across the eastern extremities of the prairie region in particular, fires or the lack of them advanced or retarded the fortunes of the prairie grasses. And to some extent the paths of fires long since dead can still be read even on the face of the high prairie landscape.

One of these places is on Buffalo Ridge, as the prairie coteau is called in southwestern Minnesota. The Chanarambie Creek cut into the landscape a gorge so narrow that the prairie fires leaped or passed around it. In the unburned depths of this gorge, a mature bur oak forest now stands. The tops of the trees do not, even today, show much above the grass-crowned ridges of the gorge, so the place is called the Lost Forest of Chanarambie.

In the beginning, the prairie fires were the work of lightning, a potent force. Across the earth, something like 100,000 lightning strikes occur every day, and perhaps a tenth of these light fires. The modern environment contains many shields against these strikes, but it was not always so. Only a little more than two centuries ago, Benjamin Franklin became the toast of Europe and America by inventing the lightning rod.

Later, the Plains Indians became agents of fire as well. Sometimes their campfires ran wild, but they had also learned how to use fires deliberately in the management of the bison, upon which they were dependent. Fires were used in the hunt to herd the bison toward kill sites. And the Indians had observed that bison tended to follow the prairie fires to take advantage of the succulent grasses that flourished in their wake. So the Indians used controlled burns to lure the herds within range. It was, in a crude sense, a kind of bison farming.

The transcontinental trains that brought settlers to the prairies rolled on iron wheels striking iron rails. The sparks that resulted set many of the prairie fires that were one of the continual terrors of pioneer life. A prairie fire could be heard, it was said, almost as soon as it could be seen, and the roar became deafening as the towering wall of flames ran nearer. To make a fire break was one of the essential skills of early prairie life.

Even after moldboard plows had broken much of the prairie sod, fire continued to shape the landscape. It was routinely employed to clear the stubble from croplands and hayfields, as it still is on the wheatlands of the high plains. When I was a boy, my family burned the meadows on our farm every fall. I didn't know then that the hayfield was a remnant of the native prairie, and I am sure that my father didn't know why fire worked there as it did, or how. He learned farming as a trade and not as a science. As I remember it, our fires were always set in the evening so that it was already dark when the last of the glowing embers in the cordgrass at the edge of the marsh had been stamped out. We children would ride the bouncing hayrack home under the stars. There would be a chill in the clean air, and we would carry the aroma of smoke with us to our beds. It was one of the particular pleasures of autumn.

Although professional managers are now experimenting with burns at other times of the year, the fires set these days on the native prairies are mainly spring fires. This is because fire is used not only to rejuvenate the vegetation but also to weed it of alien competitors. The native grasses are principally warm-season species. That is, they are generally slow to sprout, and they come to fruit in late summer or early fall when temperatures are high. The alien grasses, on the other hand, are mainly cool-season grasses; they tend to sprout early and come to fruit in late spring or early summer when temperatures are relatively cool. Controlled prairie burns are ideally timed after the alien species have sprouted but while the native grasses are still dormant, setting the early grasses back and giving the native species a better chance to attain dominance. The Compass Prairie has been managed in this way, with spectacular results.

Fire, of course, is destructive as well as beneficial, even on the prairies, but it is probably not so destructive as one might think. For one thing, a prairie fire generates intense heat, as much as 400° or 500°, but not at the level of the sod. You can safely place your palms upon the sod immediately behind the line of a prairie fire because even in the moment of burning the temperature there rarely rises above 65° F. So a spring fire has little opportunity to do damage to the living crowns of the grasses hiding in the scorched sod or the seeds waiting to sprout. Nor does it harm the many creatures that take refuge in the sod or in the earth below it: the burrowing mammals, the reptiles and amphibians, the insects in egg or pupa cases or those that lead subterranean lives. Birds and larger mammals are generally able to get out of the way. So the damage is probably limited to eggs or young birds on the nest, to immature insects, and to forbs already growing, especially those in flower.

On the presettlement prairies, when a fire might have burned hundreds of square miles at a time, presenting impenetrable walls of flame fifteen or twenty feet high and miles across, there would undoubtedly have been much more severe consequences. Such fires occasionally caught even whole herds of bison and incinerated them. But the prairie is an equation, and fire was then, as now, one critical factor in keeping it balanced.

The air in late June turned hot and stale, and in the face of it, the pace of prairie life slowed. The days were already shortening and the growing season was more than a quarter spent, but the unburned grasslands were still cloaked with the brown topdress of last year's debris and with the seedstalks of imported bluegrass. One piece of the Blue Mounds had been burned the fall before, however. I went to inspect it.

Immediately across the still-plain fire line, the cushy carpet of mulch underfoot gave way to firm earth, and the grasses, many of them native species, were green and luxuriant.

Vigorous bunches of prairie dropseed had been stimulated into life. They had a wiry and angular, an arid look (in fact, the pear cactuses nearby were in brilliant yellow and early bloom), and they danced in the breeze.

I crossed an old fenceline. The fence had been gone for five years, but its ghost lurked in the bluegrass that had choked out all native growth along its path. Another century might pass before the line of the fence was no longer visible. The prairie was created over millennia and lasted for millennia; once it was wounded, its bruises were also slow to heal.

Beyond the fence, clumps of big bluestem, the grass that gave the tallgrass prairie its name and its character, took hold. Some bunches of the grass had already blossomed, and their ovaries were plump with seed, an event that had come two months early. The fire of the previous fall had contributed to this early fecundity. Nearby a hoary puccoon and a birdsfoot violet, two of the earliest flowers of spring, were still in bloom. There is never any sharp line between one season and the next. The seasons run in one long, slow dissolve.

I stopped to admire a tall cinquefoil, an uncommon plant on the Mounds, paused to watch thousands of aphids sucking away at the stems in a patch of goldenrods. The aphids themselves were being devoured by the dozens of ladybugs that had been attracted to the feast. Farther on, I came upon the fresh mound of a badger.

Beyond that bloomed the flowers of two more species of cinquefoil; of the yarrow, our native carrot; of oxeye daisies. Great waves of purple prairie phlox splashed across the prairie.

I came again to a place where fire had not recently burned. The landscape was still brown on top but underneath it was green with a monotony of bluegrass. It was weedy. When this place had been a pasture, it had seemed to bear nothing but gumweed. It had seemed a bald and bitter place then. It had begged then for the match that would work its complicated and sometimes mysterious wonders.

6

There was a time when the booming of the prairie chickens was the first formal announcement of spring, but the grouse largely disappeared after the coming of agriculture. They were once so numerous, the young James Audubon reported, that they were "looked upon with more abhorrence than the crows." Although nobody would consider eating one, they were slaughtered in vast numbers. Moreover, they found it impossible to adjust to the loss of their native habitat. (As long as there were still unplowed hay meadows, they prospered, increased, even, after settlement.) The eastern subspecies, the heath hen, ultimately met extinction; the midwestern subspecies (*Tympanughus cupido pinnatus*) survives today only in very restricted areas under careful management and in places like Kansas where there are still large tracts of unplowed land.

So the prairies now waited in silence until the red-winged blackbirds returned. A few might arrive as early as late February, but the migration began in earnest in mid-March. The red-wings migrated in great undulating flocks. When they landed in a tree somewhere to rest, the sound of their chatter was like water falling over a long precipice, and when they took off again, the rush of their wings was like the murmur of the March wind.

The first flocks of red-wings consisted entirely of males. There might be a gap of some weeks between the arrival of the first males and the appearance of the first females. In the meantime, the males were busy on the breeding marshes establishing territorial rights. Each male's territory was an eighth to a quarter of an acre, and it was established principally in this manner: the bird took a prominent perch within the new territory, arched forward on it, and spread its wings so that its scarlet epaulets were plain to see, singing *ookalee, ookalee, ookalee* all the while. The broader the display of epaulets—a bit of macho adornment soldiers have adopted—the more passionate the singing of the song.

Sometimes two males met at a border they proposed to hold in common. There they perched, showed their epaulets, and raised their bills disdainfully into the air. Then one of them would fly haughtily off to some more central perch, while the other remained unmoved at the border.

At intervals between these basic defensive maneuvers, the male in a territorial mood would make stalling flights from perch to perch within his grounds, flashing his epaulets and spreading his tail. He might sing on these occasions, or he might not. When he did, it was with the *ookalee* song, that warm, burbling, watery call that defines the character of a marsh as much as the cattails that grow around its edges. The other basic sounds in the bird's defensive vocabulary were a harsh *check*, a warning of danger, and the *tseert*, a short, clear whistle warning more specifically of predators, particularly from the air, an alarm sufficient to bring all bird song in a marsh to an abrupt halt.

When the first females came a few weeks later, they gathered in the trees at the edge of the marsh. The males commenced immediately to solicit them. They flew back and forth before the females, making exaggerated shows of their wing colors and singing sweetly. Then each of them flew off to indicate his territory. They came back and repeated the invitation. All morning long, they importuned the females to join them. But the females flew on to another place.

New females would be arriving almost daily now, however. The small group that came the next afternoon stayed on. They went off individually to the males in their territories.

The females spent much of their time hidden among the reeds. The males pursued them there to initiate the business of mating. The opening gambit was a gesture in which the male took a perch right above the female and crouched there, issuing a series of short, high *tseetees* which sounded like whimpers. As the bonding strengthened, the pair played an aerial game of tag. The female led, flying a darting course, sometimes in, sometimes out of their territory. The male pursued, crying *tch tch tch tch* after her. He was joined briefly by several males from the neighboring territories. Eventually he caught the female and gave her a peck with his beak. They returned to their territory, he to his command post, she to her hiding place among the reeds.

The male also played a game in which he flew overhead in the vicinity of his mate, singing exuberantly, and then suddenly stretched his wings into a vee above his head and plunged into the reeds with a prolonged cry that was loud and rasping. On the ground, he waddled among the reeds with his wings still in a vee. On several occasions, the female flew to him and followed after him as he performed his antics.

When it was time to mate, both birds began to sing this whimpering song. The female crouched with her head and tail raised. She fluttered her wings. The male came with his body feathers fluffed and his tail spread. As he neared her, he, too, briefly fluttered his wings. Then he mounted her.

After they had mated, the female built a nest. She chose a place where the reeds were particularly dense, collected grasses and reeds from nearby, and wove them around three cattail stalks into a structure well hidden but high enough off the ground to be safe from flooding and somewhat protected from ground and water predators.

In the meantime, another female had arrived in her territory to share her mate. The two of them flew at each other and called to each other and snubbed each other just as the males had done weeks earlier. They subdivided the marsh territory into two lots. They were not, however, so diligent about this territory-fending as the males had been. They did not have the time. The first female had begun to lay her eggs.

She laid a total of four eggs and began to incubate them. She would get no help in this task from the male. But he did stop making feeding excursions outside his territory to assume full-time defense of his ground. From now on until their young had fledged, the two birds would eat only what they could scrounge at home. Eleven days after the incubation began, the birds hatched.

Now the female's days were occupied in keeping watch over her young birds. She carried food to them. She was encouraged in this by the bright orange color the babies flashed when they opened their beaks wide to beg. She carried away the little sacs of feces that the youngsters dropped. She stood defense against potential predators, flying off a little distance from the nest, making a racket, and flipping one or the other of her wings violently. Even if her own mate came near during one of these crises, she chased him off so that the exact location of the nest would not be revealed.

One afternoon a crow came into the marsh, intent on making a meal of the baby blackbirds. The mother, seeing the danger, left the nest and began to cry out loudly *ch ch chee-chee*, and to flick her tail. The male, roused by the warning, started to shout *check check check* over and over again, and he flicked his tail up and down. The two of them made such a commotion that the other birds in the marsh knew the nature of the danger. Males from all over the marsh responded to their cries and joined in a unified assault on the crow. They lunged at it fearlessly and repeatedly, and screamed at it with such persistence that the crow eventually decided the meal wasn't worth the effort and flew away in search of other pickings. But on other days that spring, the blackbirds would not be so triumphant.

Eleven days after they had hatched, the young blackbirds left the nest. They crawled out and perched in the grass nearby. One night a bull snake swallowed one of them. The father now took some interest in caring for his youngsters. He helped the mother feed the three birds that remained.

Eleven days after they crawled out of the nest, when it was already nearing summertime, the three fledglings were strong enough to fly. Soon they would be self-sufficient enough to fend for themselves. Then they would take leave of their home territory and fly off to join the flock of juveniles that had taken up residence at the other end of the marsh.

Once their offspring had departed, the relationship between the two adults came to an end. The female joined a flock of other mothers whose breeding duties had ended. The male, however, stayed on his territory. He had by now another nest of infants to defend.

7

Spring never seems authentic to me until the meadowlarks have returned. The wonderful, complicated song of the western meadowlark was, I suppose, the first bird song I learned, or perhaps it was only the first that I remembered. It is still one of my favorite songs.

Roger Tory Peterson, who has such a splendid gift for describing bird songs, says of the western meadowlark's in his guidebooks only that it is "variable: 7-10 notes, flutelike, gurgling and double-noted; unlike clear whistles of eastern meadowlark." But someone once described the difference between the songs of the two species more aptly: "The eastern," he said to me, "sounds like an amateur western in rehearsal."

It was the meadowlark's song that came into Willa Cather's head when she needed a title for her novel about a great soprano. In calling her book *The Song of the Lark*, Cather made the prairie roots of her art explicit. There had always been something of both love and hate in Cather's response to the world she had known as a girl in Red Cloud, Nebraska, but the love had gone disproportionately to the prairie itself. She had made a schoolgirlishly serious study of the natural history of the prairie when she was young. That she learned her lessons well is manifested in the sparkling passages of description that attend the characters in her prairie novels. Although she settled in an apartment in New York's Greenwich Village, where she could be close, among other things, to the opera she loved, it had been to the prairies of southern Nebraska that she had repaired in 1912, when she was a young woman, to make the momentous decision to be a writer. Two years later, when she took up the subject of influences that make an artist, she chose to write about a singer, and it was, perhaps, inevitable that the singer should remind her of the song of the lark. The song is, after all, the premier music of the prairies.

It is music. That is one thing. The song of the meadowlark is long enough and rich enough to be called a melody. It is rhythmic, tuneful, memorable, has dynamics, a roundness, a shapeliness that make it more than simply a characteristic succession of noises associated with a particular species of bird. The song of the western meadowlark might be used as the theme in a formal composition. It offers rich possibilities for variation; in fact, meadowlarks themselves make at least fifty variations on it.

There is also its tone, full-bodied, high, and lilting, like Rampal playing one of his Japanese melodies. There is a sharpness and clarity in it, a carrying quality that is like the flute or the tone of a bell. There is also a singing in it, which, like the sound of a violin, echoes the human voice. But the voice of a meadowlark is like the rumble of thunder or the roar of a great fall of water: it fills the landscape. Even passing in an automobile at sixty miles an hour with the windows turned up and the air conditioning running in the summertime, one can sometimes hear the song of a meadowlark. Because it is so bright and so distinct and so omnipresent, the song of the meadowlark becomes for prairie dwellers an intimacy. One gets used to it, as one gets used to the sound of a mate's breathing in the night.

A meadowlark sings to be heard. It announces its song, then waits three long beats before repeating it. It does not always sing its song in exactly the same way. It sings with double-forte conviction. It sings all the day long, from before sunrise until after sunset. In the heat of a summer afternoon, when nothing but the fata morganas stir, the cheerful melody of the meadowlark continues. What practical good can come from so much singing?

When I think of the meadowlark, I think of mornings in springtime, of the sun low on the horizon, of the long shadows that are cast; of the color yellow; of cloudless days; of air that feels on one's cheeks like the first plunge into a lake on a hot day; of the smell of mud; of rime frost on the grass.

A woman who grew up in pioneer days on the Montana grasslands once told me a story about the meadowlarks. A group of us had been talking about the effects of the landscape on human consciousness. I had said that humans, in Western cultures at least, need to take possession of spaces before they can feel comfortable in them. "A child's blanket provides security," I had said, "because it marks off a personal and therefore defensible space. The immense effort undertaken to divide the prairie into mile-square sections also seems to have been a form of taking possession. And suburban lawns and family pictures on company desks are similar acts of territoriality." "But," I had asked, "how was it possible for the pioneers to possess the vast spaces of the unsettled prairies? Didn't this immunity from possession prove terrifying to the first white settlers?"

"Not necessarily," replied the woman from Montana. "For example," she said, "where I grew up, it was our springtime custom to find, each one of us, a personal meadowlark's nest along the route to school. By spitting on the nest, it forever after became our property to watch over, to protect, to do with as we wished, and nobody else could come near it."

There might still come a spring morning when I will put on my coat and hat and go down to a remnant of the old prairies and find myself a meadowlark's nest to spit upon. Perhaps I will try someday to take possession of all the songs that might be born there.

8

I looked around, I put down my pitcher
I picked up a clumsy log
And threw it at the water-trough with a clatter.
I think it did not hit him,

But suddenly that part of him that was left behind
   convulsed in undignified haste,
Writhed like lightning, and was gone
Into the black hole, the earth-lipped fissure
   in the wall-front,
At which, in the intense still noon, I stared
   with fascination.
And immediately I regretted it.
. . .
And I wished he would come back, my snake.
For he seemed to me again like a king,
Like a king in exile, uncrowned in the underworld,
Now due to be crowned again.
And so, I missed my chance with one of the lords
   of life.
And I have something to expiate;
A pettiness.

—D. H. Lawrence
"Snake"

I had something of a mystical introduction to garter snakes. When I was a very young boy, at the impressionable age of four or five, I went for the day to the farm of an uncle to play with older cousins. The farmstead was set in an unusually large grove along a winding creek where northern pike spawned in the springtime. It was not well kept. The grove sheltered the rusting hulks of forgotten cars, which it was great fun to pretend to drive, and many pieces of abandoned farm machinery. I remember an old steam-powered tractor and a threshing rig in particular, and great piles of miscellaneous junk.

On the afternoon I am thinking of, we went down into the grove to play car. We passed from one vehicle to another, each of us taking a turn at each wheel. We came eventually to the most decrepit of the wrecks, an automobile that had given up its chassis to the construction of a farm wagon and its top to some bit of tinwork and which now consisted of little more than a set of doors and a dashboard. But the dashboard was handsomely appointed with instruments, and it had a padded steering wheel which played freely because it was not connected to anything. It was an altogether satisfying plaything. The bit of a car body sat directly upon the ground, and stinging nettles had grown up inside it. We began to beat the weeds down with sticks so that we could crawl inside.

A snake darted out from among the weeds. It stirred tremendous confusion. The older boys raised their voices. Someone gave the command to catch the thing. The creature must be caught. We made a rapid pursuit through the woods with sticks.

We caught the creature and pinned it behind its head. It was a garter snake. Its tongue darted in and out, and its eyes flashed the look of fire and fear. Someone commanded us to beat the thing into unconsciousness. We bashed away at it until there could not have been an unbattered part in its poor limp body.

But this alone would not do. The carcass could not be left. "The snake is not actually dead," the oldest cousin said. He had the manner of one who knows what he is talking about. "Hang it on a pole. Quick! We've got to get it out of here," he ordered. And so it was. We marched out of the woods carrying the snake pole on our shoulders as jungle hunters do. It was critical, according to the oldest boy, that the snake be brought immediately into full view of the sun.

He commanded that a hammer and spike be brought to him. This was done. Then, with great ceremony, he nailed the snake by its tail to a fence post in the center of the yard. It had to be a post out of any possible shadow. When he had finished, he gathered the rest of us around and told us solemnly, in the same way that his father, no doubt, had told him, that a snake would never die until it had hung by its tail in the presence of the sun going down and of the sun coming up again. "If you cross the path of a snake," he explained, "you must kill it and hang it up by its tail before sundown, or the soul of the snake will leave its body and take possession of you, and from this possession, which is the incarnation of the devil in you, there is no escape."

I half-believed that the devil lived in snakes. Was it not the serpent in the garden who had tempted Eve? But I did not have the energy or

the will to kill every snake I came across. I caught the little ones and
threw them at girls during recess. And I sat down unawares upon one
in the grass once and it bit me and the bite stung like fire. I learned
from that encounter that the garter snake has a contentious disposition
and gives off a foul odor. What's more, it isn't an amusing snake like
the puff adder. It isn't a docile and charming one like the bull snake. It
doesn't have the allure of danger, as the rattler does. What does it have
to recommend it? Why shouldn't it be an agent of the devil?

When we moved to the farm by the river, I had occasion to extend
greatly my acquaintance with garter snakes. An abandoned well in the
yard of that farmstead had been filled many years earlier with field-
stones. The well was not far from the slopes of the river bluffs, which
faced south. Garter snakes have been known to hibernate in colonies
with populations as high as 10,000, and they come back to the same
dens year after year. Our well was one of their hibernacula.

In the spring, the garter snakes would begin to emerge from the den.
There would be a mass of them the first day sunning on the rotting
pump platform. Every day after that, a few more would emerge. They
would spill out onto the grass at the base of the platform. I learned to
keep a sharp watch when I was walking barefooted in the neighborhood of the well in the springtime.

The numbers of the snakes and the frantic activity were awesome,
and the event was puzzling because it lasted so long. One would have
thought that after a winter of hibernation the snakes would go directly
off into the wide world, in search of food and water if nothing else.

In a week or two, they would leave, but they never went far at first;
I could always find them basking in the sun on the hillside just below
the well. There might be two or three of them in a rather tight group,
but generally when the snakes went to the hillside, they spread themselves out, took on a more solitary way of life. Still, there were enough
of them and the area they occupied was small enough so the entire
hillside seemed alive with snakes.

After that, the snakes dispatched to the far corners of the farm
and were never again so active or so visible. I would see one now and

again in the grass—but always by chance. I didn't know, as I did with many other creatures, exactly where to go to find a snake. Sometimes I would come across the shed skin of one along a pasture path. In late August, when the babies first appeared, the snakes became a bit more visible again, but it was never anything like the situation in spring-time. And then one fall day, they would return to the well and bed down for the winter, although exactly when the migration took place, I couldn't say. I never saw it.

Many years after I had left the farm, I learned what my garter snakes were doing at the old well in the early spring. They were reproducing. The mass of snakes around the entrance to the well was a mating ball.

Mating in garter snakes of the North (there are species of them everywhere on the continent) is temperature-regulated. A garter snake in this respect is a little like a tulip bulb. The males will not breed unless they have been exposed to temperatures of less than 10° C for at least seven weeks; nor will they breed until the tempera-ture is at least 25° C.

When the temperature in spring has reached a suitable level and the mayonnaise-thick blood of the snakes has thinned again and their bodies have adjusted physiologically in other ways to the coming of spring, the males shake hibernation and emerge all at once from the den. For some reason of instinct or habit, they do not immediately leave for their summer grounds, but linger to await the emergence of the females, which soon begin to stir. The females leave the den singly or in small groups.

When a female garter snake comes out into the open after a win-ter of hibernation, she will be mobbed by tens or hundreds of would-be suitors. She will have secreted through her skin a pheromone—a chemical substance manufactured in this case in the blood—which drives the males into a frenzy of sexual passion. The same chemical triggers the synthesis of yolk. The quantity of the pheromone that is produced depends to some extent on the number of eggs the snake laid the year before. So the most fecund snakes are the most attractive to potential mates and the most likely to be impregnated. In the natural world, fecundity is its own reward. If mating doesn't occur, no yolks are produced; the garter snake does most of its living in the three or four months of summer, and it would be profligate to spend resources during those months on eggs that are unlikely to be fertile.

One snake in the writhing ball of males is soon in a position to mate. When this happens, the reproductive parts of the two creatures literally lock together. The female controls the action once a pair is fastened. Mating takes about fifteen minutes. During that time, the male deposits in the female a gelatinous plug, which not only mechanically frustrates further mating but also exudes a second pheromone, manufactured by the male, which renders her sexually unattractive. Once this mating plug is inserted, the creatures detach, and the female leaves immediately for her summer grounds, which may be as many as eight or nine miles away.

The mating plug in the female considerably enhances her chances of survival. During mating, the female is vulnerable to attack by crows, which prey at the dens in the springtime, attracted by the prospect of getting a delectable bit of snake liver. The plug guarantees that she will be mated only once, thus minimizing this risk. The sooner the female mates and gets on her way, the higher are the odds that she, and the species with her, will survive.

Snakes were once a regular part of my life. Then came a time when I hardly ever saw them. During my snakeless period, I had a nightmare. I dreamed that I and my mother and my sister were trapped in a pit of some kind at the edge of a lake and that a tremendous storm had suddenly come up which prevented us from going out into the open. I dreamed that the three of us gradually realized that the pit was actually a snake den and that we were steadily sinking into the depths of it. The level of the snakes writhing and churning against our bodies rose higher and higher. At the moment when I awoke, we were about to be suffocated in the press of snakes.

I did not know about mating balls in garter snakes then, although I had watched them many times without knowing what I was seeing, but when I thought about it the next morning, I presumed that the snakes in my dream were garter snakes.

I could make no sense of the dream, didn't want to actually. It never came back again, and it seemed on its surface to be the kind of dream that could well turn out to have humiliating interpretations. Nevertheless, I told it one night to a writer who took her Jung and her dreams very seriously. I told it to her because it had surprised me by insinuating itself in a story I was writing.

"Oh, yes! Yes!" she said. "Snakes in the basement, yes! Weak fathers, yes, and little boys struggling against the devils. In vain! In vain! Yes, in vain!"

So the business of snakes came down in the end to deviltry after all.

9

There seems in late spring to be an openness, a frankness, a guilelessness that is missing at other times of the year. I do not suppose that there is more to this than an impression. Life is never innocent.

But there is in spring the openness of the landscape itself. The trees, although green, are not yet in full leaf. One can still see sky through the canopy of a tree. In the grasslands, the vegetation has begun to green, the earliest of the flowers are in bloom, the insects are about, the spiders are at their webs, the music of the birds is in the air. Everywhere there is the motion of life as it has not been evident for months. But the grasses are just sprouting, and even the fastest growing of the forbs is yet a diminutive thing. The dense thicket of prairie growth has not yet been formed in late spring. One can still see through the shoots of things to the surprisingly bare prairie floor.

Young birds are in the shell or on the nest or they are fledgling. Despite the cleverness with which they have been domiciled, the persistent wanderer cannot help but stumble upon them. The same is true for the young of the mammals. It takes time and attention to catch a fox in action at any other time of the year, but in spring, even a modestly observant dilettante can find the occupied den of one and stake it out. There is too much youthfulness about life in the spring to keep it long hidden.

So it was that while wandering along a prairie lane one late spring evening, I came to spend a quarter of an hour in the company of a badger. I was minding my own business. I was tired and on my own time. I was not about to get into communion with anything. I simply wanted quiet and the relaxation of being aimlessly in motion.

I had gone a mile or a little more. I was beyond sight and sound of the prairie village in which I lived. The night was springishly free from pollen and insect pests. I was caught up in the absence of my own thoughts. The fact of a world beyond the extremities of my own body had entirely escaped me.

And then it aroused me—as if it were a bar of music to which I was awakening—a loud rustling in the grass at my side. It frightened me. It was such a strange, disembodied, improbably loud rustling. I stood at roadside listening for the noise in the grass again, mildly annoyed to have been interrupted so.

The rustling came again, the same loud, strange, ominous sound. It came from the bottom of the road ditch not more than ten feet away. A ripple of young grass ran up to the edge of the gravel road like a wave of water released somehow from the bondage of gravity.

From it emerged in a moment a young badger. The badger has a reputation for meanness. When it is confronted by a human, it will sometimes bare its big carnassials and begin to hiss and snarl in a most convincing manner, and it will lunge at the intruder as if to kill. A badger is not a tiny creature—an adult weighs about twenty-five pounds—and it comes low-slung, broad-skulled, pug-nosed. It is as muscled as a boxer, and it is decorated with a white racing stripe down the center of its head. It looks like a fat little bomb.

Those who have stood their ground (I am not among them) report that the badger is more bluff than bite, however. It might not stop until it is an inch and three quarters from your ankles, but it will stop.

What looks menacing in an adult often seems merely amusing in a youngster. So it was with the infant badger I was now confronting toe to toe. Its funny black and white face, its short little ears, its short little legs, its enormous, bright, black eyes—all made it seem amusing, vulnerable, appealing.

The badger took no notice of me, although once or twice it almost bumped into me. It would come to the top of the road, flop onto its belly, tuck in its legs, and slide down the young grass into the ditch. When it had reached the bottom, it would flop about until it had found its balance again, right itself, scramble back up the bank, and slide down all over again. It looked as if it was having a wonderful time.

We humans, in our thirst for exotica, like to imagine that we alone have contrived aesthetic pleasures. But it is impossible to listen to a coyote singing at moonrise or to watch a flock of swallows on the wing or to encounter a young badger at play without believing that joy is as much a biological fact of life as any other.

I, at any rate, catching the mood of the badger, went on my way again with a skip and a hop.

10

I was at the Sunrise Prairie one windy afternoon, intent upon finding a particular flower, when I was startled by the bolting of a bird. I started, looked up to see a mourning dove fleeing to a telephone wire, and scarcely avoided crushing the two tiny white eggs resting in a make-shift grass receptacle at my feet. Because it was the middle of the day, the egg-sitter was probably the father.

In the marshes, the female blackbirds were on their impossible and nearly invisible nests among the rushes, and the male blackbirds were busy fending off every invader, friendly or dangerous.

It was the season of the year when the reptiles made themselves apparent. Coming down to the edge of a prairie pond at this time of year, one almost inevitably surprised a garter snake. If it was near enough to the water, it would slip in and disappear with astonishing speed, leaving not so much as a telltale ripple on the surface. If it was on higher ground, it would dart away into the undercover of mulch and hide there until the danger had passed. At the appearance of a human invader, the mud turtles that had been taking the sun would slide down from the half-submerged trunk of a willow tree into the murky cover of the waters, and the heads of the snapping turtles, barely visible at the center of the pond, would recede silently from view. The chatter of frogs and crickets would halt. A blackbird would take to the air and begin to scold. It was like a curtain suddenly crashing down on the drama.

A calf had just been born in the pasture across the way. It raised its head and seemed to be alive. Its mother licked it and tried to get it to stand. It wouldn't or couldn't. The mother cried to it. I went off to look at other things, and when I came back, the calf's mother had left it behind, and it seemed to be dead. The calf made a blue shadow on the hillside.

The lacy baskets of the tent caterpillars adorned the branches of every plum tree. The caterpillars were early, as everything was after the mild winter, and fewer of them had emerged than might have if the winter had been longer and colder. Tent caterpillar eggs need a good, hard, prolonged freezing to hatch best. If you leave some indoors where it is cozy all winter long, they will not hatch at all.

The tents of the caterpillars got bigger as the days passed and as the moth larvae grew. Each tent held many of them. In four to six weeks, the caterpillars would be mature, and they would leave the tent for solitary lives elsewhere. By and by, each of those that survived would make cocoons, and after another winter, the cocoons would emerge as moths, which would lay eggs. After still another winter had passed, there would be tents again.

But a great many of the caterpillars would not survive the birds, and perhaps the intervening years would be abnormally warm or abnormally cold and many of them would die of exposure.

In fields and along city streets wherever I looked, there were the carcasses of the birds that had not lived. The maggots had gotten into some of them, and those that had fallen prey to predators were remembered only because of the telltale clutches of feathers that remained here and there. Even now, death was always lurking in the shadows.

It was, at last, the time of the flowers. The open prairies bloomed with birds-foot violet, Missouri violet, northern bog violet, prairie smoke, golden Alexanders, lousewort, hoary puccoon, rue anemone, false rue anemone, false Solomon's seal, leadplant, wild strawberry, chokecherry and blue-eyed grass, among others.

From now until autumn, there would be every few days and then every day, a new kind of blossom on the prairie.

Summer

1

The prairie landscape is so completely dominated by its skies that sometimes there seems to be no middle ground between us and the firmament.

There are summer days when the blue of the prairie sky permeates everything, when land and plants and air and water seem all to be molded from an identical blue material. The air on such days shimmers; it is difficult to say precisely where the horizon quits and the heavens begin.

Whirligigs dance through on such days, rustling plants and twirling dust, and making the physical reality of matter—that it is forever in motion—seem not only technically but emotionally true.

The pavement ahead along the highway, the tilled fields to the right and to the left, the grain elevators in villages along the way, everything seems to be in puddles, as after a long shower.

When a storm comes on a summer afternoon, it comes shrouded in dramatic black curtains, and after it has passed, it admits the sun which presents itself in great beams between the trailing clouds. When the sky is cloudless on a fair summer day, it is spectacularly empty. When the sky is clouded on such a day, it is just as spectacularly full. The clouds then are the high, billowy cumulus clouds, the cauliflower clouds, the heralds of balmy weather. When these clouds sit on the horizon, they look like mountain ranges. Children demand to be driven to them.

The sunrises of summer are spectacular. The sunsets of summer are spectacular. Everything about the summer sky is spectacular, showy, theatrical. The stars in the evening, the moons at midnight, the rays of the morning sun—they all shine with special brilliance.

In summer, the waters of the lakes and ponds mirror the clouds by day, the moon by night. The fireflies in the grass repeat the stars above. The drops of the dew catch and magnify the rays of the morning sun. All the prairie world is in summer but a screen to show off the glorious sky.

2

There were once tens of thousands of potholes across the prairies, but almost all of them were drained of their water over the years and the land was put to agricultural uses. They attracted breeding waterfowl by the millions. A pair of ducks could always find a suitable place in the grass near a temporary pond for a nest, and the pond could generally be counted on to serve as a refuge for the callow ducklings until they had their feathers and were capable of fending for themselves.

The shallow waters of the temporary ponds warmed quickly. Many forms of microscopic life flourished in this warmth, and the microscopic life, with the droppings of the ducks and the organic wastes that the rainwater washed into the pools, provided sustenance for the crustaceans which made the temporary ponds a way of life.

There were the little one-eyed *Cyclops,* whose females carried saddlebags of eggs. Some of them got from temporary pond to temporary pond on the currents of the winds. When a pool of water dried up, they encased themselves in cysts. The cysts either protected them until the next rainfall or rendered them transportable.

There were the fairy shrimp, which came in a variety of bright colors—blue-green, orange, red. They managed to exist everywhere, even in the most ridiculously temporary of aquatic environments, in road ditch puddles among other places. The fairy shrimp had many leaf-like legs, and they glided about on their backs by gracefully waving their comely legs. The stirrings of those legs brought to them a flow of water which ran through their mouths and was strained there of its edibles: bits of algae; one-celled protozoa and flagellates; rotifers; bacteria; bits of organic matter; microscopic fungi, ghostly and parasitic because they lacked the chlorophyll necessary to synthesize sustenance for themselves. The fairy shrimp were masterfully equipped for the art of survival. Their reproduction favored females, which could lay a clutch of as many as 250 eggs as often as every two days. These eggs had to be partially developed before they could be fully laid. They came in two varieties. There was a thin-shelled kind suitable for the high breeding season— May through early summer. And there was a thick-shelled kind which protected the embryo through such hardships as ice and drought.

Tadpole shrimp resided in the temporary ponds in vast numbers. They survived from wet season to wet season as eggs and gave to the prairie a touch of the sea: they looked like the tiny horseshoe crabs that abound on saltwater beaches. The tadpole shrimp had a taste for many things. They subsisted chiefly on microscopic organisms, but they also ate eggs as they were available. When a creature occupied a niche as chancy as the one the tadpole shrimp did, it was healthy not to be too finicky.

There were water fleas with pale yellow blood and big oval hearts and outsized compound eyes. They had long antennae which propelled them about. Almost all of the water fleas that first appeared in a pond in spring were females. Their lives were spent in a series of molts. There were several molts from hatching to adulthood, which commenced with the first brood of eggs. After that, an adult female might molt twenty-five more times, each time producing still another batch of as many as forty eggs. As spring wore on, a few males began to appear in the broods. It was not clear what brought them there. Perhaps it was a critical water temperature, perhaps overcrowding and its attendant shortage of food, perhaps a buildup of excrement—maybe all of these factors came into play. Whatever, the appearance of the males in significant numbers happened as the females were starting to produce fewer eggs. These the males fertilized. The brood chamber in which the fertilized eggs developed thickened and darkened. At the next molt, the chamber dropped away from the female into the bottom mud. It was highly resistant to drying and freezing. If there should be water again in the fall in the temporary ponds, the eggs would hatch, and the sequence would repeat itself. There would be an increase in populations until males were produced, and these would fertilize eggs that would fall away from the brood chamber and remain safe in the mud over winter, ready to hatch with the first rains of spring. If there were no fall rains, the eggs from the spring broods were equipped to last through the winter.

The same temporary waters that produced the teeming populations of one-celled animals and the rich variety of crustaceans that fed upon them, and which offered refuge for growing ducks, were also nursery chambers for the nymphal stages of many insects, of mayflies, of dragonflies, of damselflies, of mosquitoes and midges and gnats. When these insects had metamorphosed into adults, they took to the air or crawled out upon the land and became part of the chain of life beyond the waters.

There were the tadpoles of spadefoot toads in the temporary ponds. They were creatures with a genius for surviving drought. One cousin lived on the southwestern deserts in places where the rains were so scarce that there might be pools of water adequate for breeding only once every couple of years. The desert toads survived by burrowing deep into the ground before the onset of the summer heat. There they found both much cooler temperatures and some moisture that they could use, and they conserved such moisture as they had by growing a protective sheath of dead skin and by retaining their urine so as not to lose its water content. Because the spadefoot toads were dependent upon temporary pools for breeding, pools which might dry up at any time, they were able to reproduce in a hurry. A male led the way out of the underground chambers. When he reached the surface, he let out a call so commanding that all the other toads within some hundreds of yards responded. They marched en masse to the pool and mated there. Within forty-eight hours, the eggs had hatched, and in another sixteen days the first young adults were ready to leave for land. But the temporary ponds were drying up early this season, and life crowded in them. So the young tadpoles turned upon each other. When their numbers had been reduced by half, those that remained accelerated their development. The first of them were ready to begin their adult life as burrowers in the grasslands only twelve days after hatching.

The tiger salamanders had also gone in companies to the ponds in spring to mate and to deposit their eggs. The eggs had incubated for more than a month before the water temperature was right for hatching.

They had spent another month and a half in the water as larvae before achieving adulthood. Then they, like so many other pond creatures, left the water and came out to chains of life on the land. For the salamanders, life on land was lived mainly at night and mainly underground.

The Crustaceans, toads, salamanders, ducks drew sustenance from the smaller creatures which found life possible in the accumulated melts and rains of the prairie spring. These creatures would in turn feed on insects and play host to parasites and graze grasses that would become the sources of energy for bigger predators on the grass-lands. And the largest predators and the great herbivores, the bison and the elk and the antelope, would in their turn become ill and die from the advanced forms of the parasites that had begun their lives in the tiny creatures of the temporary ponds. When the creatures at the top of the food chain had fallen, their remains would be broken down by the hosts of scavengers, and the carcasses and excrement that the scavengers produced would be washed away the next spring into the temporary ponds again, and the whole cycle would begin anew.

In the meantime, the ponds that were now almost dry had served to keep the rainwaters of spring at hand, not only to fuel the cycle of energy transfers, but also to feed the water table that flowed beneath the grasses. The underground reservoir kept the level of moisture in the subsoil high even while the topsoil was crumbling into dust. It was on that subsoil moisture that the deep-rooted prairie perennials survived drought.

But the prairie world is now crisscrossed by a labyrinth of tiles and drainage ditches. Its ponds don't hold water anymore. With the disappearing ponds have vanished many of the waterfowl, many of the insects, many of the predators. The great herbivores have long since disappeared. It is by now a pale ghost of the world that once existed in this place.

3

The day dawned in a crimson blaze of sunlight. The sunlight looked red because the air was full of droplets of dust which refracted it before it reached the land. On 70 percent of the days that dawned this way, rain fell.

As the barometric pressure fell, the humidity level rose. Already the day seemed unpleasantly warm. There was an uncomfortable close-ness and stillness in the air. In the sky there were many small cumulus clouds. They accumulated throughout the morning, and some of the smaller clouds began to combine into larger ones. The surface of the earth heated unevenly. The air at ground level was cooler on the hill-tops than in the swales. An updraft of warm air began to be lifted under the pressure of the colder air.

The prairie creatures could sense that something violent was in the making. The thirteen-striped ground squirrels retreated to their dens. The red-winged blackbirds took shelter among the cattails' reeds. The muskrats sought refuge in their houses. The white-tailed deer bedded down in the oak grove. The salamanders and turtles dug into the mud at the bottom of the marsh. The nesting birds shifted in their places. The bumblebees flew home to their nests. The meadowlarks aban-doned the telephone wires and hid among the branches of the lilacs. The insects paused, quit their music. Silence came over the land. It was like the taking of a sharp breath.

The draft of warm air began to gush upward at a speed of sixty miles an hour. The water droplets cooled as they sped into the upper atmo-sphere, got heavier, combined to make bigger droplets, fell back to-ward earth, warmed as they fell, rose again on the power of the colder air lingering at ground level. Several updrafts and downdrafts began to flow within the cloud. The cloud grew bigger and bigger, taking the hulking black shape of a cumulonimbus cloud. It now extended two miles wide and seven miles high, and it began to flatten at the top, resembling a gigantic anvil. It was shortly to become a terrible instru-ment of violence.

The color of the sky deepened as the black hulk of the thunder-cloud took dominion over the landscape. It turned a brilliant Dresden blue, and against it the shiny unmoving leaves of the cottonwoods emitted an unearthly green glow, like that of the satin leaves of fairy-tale trees. The intensity of the colors magnified the stillness that had fallen over the land. The dragonflies and the butterflies had gone away somewhere. Even the gnats had fallen out of swarm. The leaves of the plant had begun to droop upon their stems in the humid depression chamber beneath the stormcloud.

The cloud grew to thirty miles across, and it reached nine and a half miles into the upper atmosphere. The temperature at the top of the cloud was −80° F. The drops of water were freezing there before they tumbled back down into the maelstrom at the center of the cloud. The forces unleashed in the cloud were now equivalent to the energy released by the explosions of nine Hiroshima-sized atom bombs.

There was a flash of lightning and the distant rumble of thunder. The cloud had become polarized. It was now manufacturing not only mighty winds and torrential rains and hail, but bolts of electricity, each with a charge of 100 million volts and an internal temperature of 50,000° F, five times the surface temperature of the sun itself.

Out of the awful silence, a faint stirring of breeze announced itself in the rustlings of the cottonwood leaves. The breeze was cool. Enough ice now filled the thunderhead so that some of the cold air from the violent upper atmosphere did not warm sufficiently in the miles it plunged toward earth to make the trip back up on the updraft. The air had leaked from the bottom of the cloud. The spill of cold air became a torrent. The malevolent, icy gusts of a thunderstorm before the rain were unleashed. They picked up the water on the surface of the marsh and whipped it into sheets of spray. The ducks hurried toward shelter in the waving reeds; the blackbirds hunkered farther down. The tops of the trees twisted and thrashed. A large limb of a cottonwood split from the main trunk and crashed to earth. A cottontail rabbit hiding in a thicket at the base of the tree was struck by the falling limb and crushed to death. The friction of the wind against the obstructions of the writhing plants made a howling. The whole earth shrieked.

There was a brief pause in the howling, and in that instant the first droplets of cold rain, broken apart and slowed on their way down in collisions with the masses of warmer air still surging upward, fell upon the earth again and broke apart altogether. The first patter of rainfall against earth sounded slow, methodical, almost mechanical. After the long breathless wait, the coming of this inevitability seemed a relief.

Then came a great flash of lightning and a terrible crack of thunder at close range, and the water in the cloud washed down in continuous sheets. It made the sound of water falling upon water. The raccoon hiding in the abandoned badger den at the edge of the marsh was forced out by the rising level of the water. The rain poured down so heavily that it clogged his nostrils. The passageways of the harvester ant den became waterlogged and began to collapse into a gooey mess. The eggs and larval cases of many insects were washed out of the grass and into the rivulets of water that flowed down the hillsides and into the ravines that ran away to the creeks, to the marshes and lakes. The carcasses of insects, the young of several nests of mice, the webs and bodies of spiders, the drowned remains of earthworms that had been driven out of their chambers by the flood were washed away into agricultural drain tiles and carried underground into drainage ditches and washed away toward the sea.

The young of some ground nesting birds were drowned. In the chambers of the ground squirrels, a few of the young drowned. The nests in the treetops were shaken loose and fell to the ground, and their eggs smashed and the yolks ran away in the deluge.

In the reeds, blackbirds drowned. Their nests collapsed on their flimsy moorings and were swept away. The water of the marsh riled under the fierce pounding of the rains and the violent whippings of the wind. Minnows and bullheads and frogs and salamanders and crayfish and snails and water insects of many kinds were carried up into the waters now choked with mud and debris, and, finding themselves unable to breathe in the muck, some of them died.

At the far edge of the marsh, a tremendous bolt of lightning brightened the whole landscape, made rivers and canyons of light in the black sky, and then crashed into the tallest cottonwood. The top half of the tree fell away, carrying with it a nest of young crows. Their mother tried desperately to keep afloat in the downpour.

And then the ice, which had been slowly losing its upward momentum as the energy in the cloud spent itself, was released and fell upon the earth as hail. It stunned a small bird into unconsciousness, pelted to death a young rabbit that cowered on its nest, stripped trees of their leaves. The hail smashed the stems of many flowering plants into the mud, knocked many green plums from their branches, stripped the early-season grasses of seeds, killed a snake and a frog. The ice accumulated in some places in drifts, looking like a fall of snow out of season.

The cooling effect of the ice robbed the thunderhead of its energy, and the great engine of violence sputtered. The fall of the rain lightened. There was a last rumble of thunder. The rain stopped. The cloud began to break up again into smaller cumulus clouds, and through the breaks in them streamed the rays of the afternoon sun. The storm had not drained the air of all of its water vapor. The temperature immediately rose, and the humidity grew heavy again. Through the dense cover of droplets, the sky became intensely blue. Across it, stretching from horizon to horizon, a full rainbow appeared. The sunlight gathered intensity. The rainbow began to fade. It slipped away altogether. There was the soft sound of water dripping. It was suddenly a peaceful summer afternoon.

As the load of water fell from the plants, the bent stems of some of them began to straighten. The ants scurried about seeking to assess the damage to their chambers and to begin the cleanup and repair. The seeds they had stored deep underground would be safe. Only a few of them had gotten damp, and none of them would sprout. The ants had bitten the radicle from each seed before putting it away so that it could not germinate. The earthworms began to dig new chambers.

Bits of egg yolk dripped into the cattail beds. Loads of silt sifted to the bottom of the marsh. Quantities of dead snails and fish fry and tadpoles were seized by colonies of scavenger bacteria. Flies began to deposit their eggs in the carcass of a raccoon. Within hours the maggots would hatch and have a go at the remains. The thread worms had already arrived and begun their work. The process of decay and renewal was in motion.

The smell of wet hair and drying feathers hung in the air. There was the odor of ozone, the sweet stench of wet earth.

In the meadow, the widowed crow flew aimlessly about. In the plum thicket, the cottontail rabbit licked her dead youngster. In the den beneath the brush pile on the far side of the meadow, the weasel ate her lost kittens.

As the darkness began in its subtle way to fall, as the sky began to redden again, as the singing of the frogs commenced, there was everywhere confusion and disarray on the prairie. In the distance, a faint rumble of thunder sounded, but it came from the east. Tomorrow would be hot and clear.

4

It did not rain again for thirty-seven days. It took some time for the consequences of this to be felt. The snows of winter had been plentiful, and they had melted gradually. There had been spring showers. And the thunderstorm had deposited more than four inches of rain. Almost half of that had collected on leaves of various kinds and had evaporated during the first warm, bright days after the storm. Still, the soil was moist all the way up to its surface.

In the first week and a half after the storm, growth and flowering flourished as usual. The cool-season grasses—June grass, Canada wild rye, western wheatgrass, needle-and-thread grass—were all green with new growth and in full flower. They were irresistible now to the grazers. The prairie beans were developing fruits; the ground plums were showing the first tinges of rose on their fat lime-colored fruits; the aromatic prairie sage had turned silvery green and showed on the hillsides in bright patches. The landscape was by now predominantly green, but it was still peppered with the brown stems of the warm-season grasses which were just getting their first big spurt of growth.

The temperatures after the storm climbed to unseasonable heights. They averaged in the upper nineties during the days, and they did not fall far at night, often no farther than the low eighties. With the relative humidity at not much more than 30 percent, there was little water vapor in the air to diffuse the merciless fall of the light. But the atmosphere was still turbid with particles of dust. Every cubic foot of the air contained billions of them. There was never a moment, even in the middle of a rainstorm, when they were not there. As many as were washed away in one fall of rain were accumulated in some dry place elsewhere upon the earth. They returned on the winds that forever swirled, even as they were now swirling about and sucking up the prairie's moisture and carrying it off to other places. It was the dust that made the water in the ponds and the air in the sky look blue. Overhead, the dust filtered out the reds, greens, and violets from the light, leaving visible only the blue end of the spectrum. It also screened out some of the warmth in the light. Without the haze of dust in which the prairie was enveloped, the heat of the drought would have been even more unbearable. It was the dust that made the sunrises and sunsets look orange and red because at the angle of the horizon, it filtered the blues out of the light. Without the dust the drought would have gone on forever. It was around one of its particles that every drop of rain and every crystal of snow was made.

There were no clouds, none of the picturesque cottonballs of summer, so there was no shade from the clouds. There was seldom even one of those passing flights of shadow and breeze that play across a benign July or August landscape. There was a steady wind, but it came from the southwest and it blew hot and dry.

The high temperatures, the cloudless skies, the hot southwest winds began to take their toll. It was the time of year when the expenditure of water in the manufacture of topgrowth is immense. The additional payment of water in transpiration and evaporation soon began to exhaust the earth's reserves.

Two weeks into the dry spell, the surface soil crumbled underfoot. When the wind gusted, it stirred up clouds of dust. A farmer working in his fields was now tracked by the cloud of dust that followed him, like the contrail of jet, for half a mile or more. Half a foot down into the earth, however, there was still plenty of moisture.

The sprouted grass seedlings, equipped only with flimsy surface roots, wilted as the dryness continued, and at three weeks, most of them were dead. Not many of them would have lived anyway. The established plants were already tall enough to shade them, robbing them of adequate sunlight, and the food stocks in the seeds from which they had sprouted were already exhausted. On some of the dry and gravelly knolls, the alien stands of invading bluegrass were beginning to be stressed in the middle of the day. The native junegrass was also beginning to suffer. The young plants of the chief domesticated grass, corn, had begun to curl upon themselves in the afternoons to conserve their moisture. Most of the native grasses, however, could cope. They were mainly perennials with deep roots.

At the beginning of the fourth week of the drought, the moisture reserves in the first foot of earth were spent. In places where the soil had been waterlogged and was badly aerated, cracks began to open in the surface of the earth.

The water level in the ponds and marshes steadily dropped. The spring pools of water among the rocks on top of the Blue Mounds dried up. So did the shallow temporary ponds in the bottom lands.

By the fifth week of the drought, there was no moisture at all in the first couple of feet of soil and below that moisture was also rapidly disappearing. For some plants, it was already too late to be saved by rain. Many of the invading bluegrass plants had now died, and so had many of the junegrass plants. Their brown top growth showed prominently now on the summer landscape. On the rocky ledges of the Blue Mounds and on the knolls of the Cayler Prairie, the bunches of blue gama grass and buffalo grass had already entered dormancy. Individual stiff sunflower and coneflower plants were wilted or browning.

But other plants had adjusted their priorities to meet the challenge. The big bluestem, the goldenrods, the milkweeds, the many-flowered asters had all rushed their flowers into production. The prairies looked two or three weeks farther along than they ought to have at this time of the year. Some of the flowers prospered and produced early seeds, if somewhat smaller than normal. These seeds were insurance against the possibility of long-term drought. Other early flowers withered and died without ever coming to fruit. They were all the flowers of perennials, which, if the drought was not too severe, would come back from their roots in the next season anyway. Simply to be done with flowering was an advantage under the circumstances.

Once flowering was at an end, the plants could concentrate on building up reserves of carbohydrates, nitrogen, and minerals for use next spring. In autumn, these excess nutrients would be translocated from the leaves and stems to the roots and rhizomes below ground for storage through the long winter.

The thick stands of cordgrass along the rims of the low places were always prepared for drought. They needed lots of water to support their tremendous height, but, even in years of normal rainfall, the water in the upper levels of the soil would eventually dry up in the places they preferred. So cordgrass plants put down deep roots from the start. Now, however, sensing extraordinary stress, the cordgrass plants stopped their top growth and began instead to extend their sixteen-foot roots even deeper into the subsoil.

Generally across the prairies, the growth of the plants stopped. Growth required water, and none was available, at least near the surface. The grasses that could curled their leaves up to slow the rate of water loss in the heat and glare of midday. Plants whose leaves had no mechanisms for curling closed down their stoma and allowed their leaves to droop away from the direct sunlight. Many plants began to shed leaves. They were not needed now to supply the engines of growth and flowering, and they would transpire some precious water if they remained.

As spare leaves fell away, and annual plants died, and flowers withered, and cool-season grasses turned brown, the prairie came to seem thin and brittle. My footsteps raised a bit of dust and crunched now when I went out walking in the grasslands. It was like walking across the prevernal prairie. A greater surface of the earth was exposed now to the scorching rays of the sun than would have been exposed in a year when the rains had fallen in usual volume. The drought began to feed upon itself. On the open land, the soil temperature mounted abnormally, the humidity level fell abnormally, and these developments set the stage for a further attrition of vegetation and, in turn, for a higher extreme of drought.

Life of every kind became more constricted. Insects rushed the production of eggs for the coming year and hurried through their own lives.

When they had a choice, animals chose to be about at night when it was cooler rather than in the daytime. Burrowing animals bedded down as much as they could in their soil-cooled burrows. Turtles and toads dug into the mud. Earthworms descended deeper into the earth, and when the soil began to dry out even a yard down, many of them lapsed into a state of torpor and commenced to wait the drought out. The crop of young earthworms would be extremely small this year.

On the marshes, the boundaries of the water shrank and its depth dwindled. Life grew crowded in the muskrat communities, and as the crowding worsened, a general irritability set in. The young muskrats began to pick fights with the older ones. On the marsh at Rush Lake half a dozen muskrats were nursing deep gash wounds, and one old and feeble muskrat bled to death from the wounds he had suffered in a scrap with an out-of-sorts youngster. One of the juveniles set out for a new territory and was killed as he tried to cross the highway. Another wandered without eating for three days and then was set upon by a mink as he lay sleeping in the open; the mink killed him before he had awakened enough to put up much of a struggle.

On the Blue Mounds, the bison rolled over and over again in the dust in a vain effort to rid themselves of the hordes of insect pests that were feeding upon them. They scratched themselves with their sandpaper tongues until they opened bleeding sores upon their backs. The friskiness of the calves came to be an annoyance to the cows. More than one of them got a harder butt on the head than it deserved.

The monotonous heat and light of the drought fostered lethargy and anger. Every creature felt these countervailing forces. The birds, the bees, the insects, I myself, grew listless and cranky. There was a dizziness about it. The whole world seemed to shimmer sickeningly in and out of focus even as the waves of heat writhed up into the oppressive air. There was a mean and unforgiving edge in the drought, and the cut of it was beginning to be felt at every hour of the day and night.

I remembered going home again in another year after a long absence and finding the land clutched in the suffocating embrace of a long drought. I had returned for sentimental reasons; I had wanted to show a friend the place of my upbringing. It must have been in late

July. A pitiful harvest of small grains was being gathered in, and the farmers were thankful for it. There was going to be nothing else to harvest that year.

The channels in which the streams had run were now merely gullies. They were like the cracks that open in the soles of the barefooted in the summertime. The swales in which there had been marshes were now hard gray lesions rent with a labyrinth of cracks. The rents in the earth ran through the long fields of corn and soybeans. It was plain how much the soil resembled skin. As it dried and cracked open, the earth itself seemed senescent.

The soybean plants had sprouted and grown for a while. Some of them reached nearly a foot in height before they had died. They stood now as incongruous rows of sticks in the gray earth. In the ghost cornfields, there was a straggly plant every eight or ten feet, ankle high, leaning with the wind and dragging its limp leaves upon the earth. The fields seemed poorer for the few survivors. Had nothing lived, there might at least have been the illusion that nothing had, after all, been planted.

There was a gentle wind. It was stirring up the bits of soil that had fractured into a fine dust and was lifting them into the air. They turned the sky the ashen color of a person with a terminal disease. It was almost 100°F. My neck and brow were covered with sweat, and where there was sweat, the film of dust in the air had been drawn to it as ink is to blotting paper. I was stained with the fragments of my broken homeland. They dug and cut into the folds of my neck.

Perhaps it is inexact to describe the color of things as gray. It was true that when the moisture had gone out of the earth, which lay everywhere exposed in its sickness like a patient, the earth had lost its blackness and become a thing nondescript, some faint semblance of black. Perhaps it is more accurate to describe the color of the parched land as yellow. The shriveled grass in the road ditches was yellow, and the wide and thin winnows of threshed grain straw were yellow, and a yellow showed in the leaves of the trees, and the sky itself had a thick and bitter, a bilious look, a yellowness. There was the color of resignation in the landscape. Such resistance as endured lay smoldering beneath a yellow flag.

Already the looters and rioters of the plant world had come out. The first of the Russian thistles, the tumbling tumbleweeds, had begun to roll across the land, scattering their opportunistic little seeds far and wide. There was a place along the road to the old farm where the earth had begun to run like a drift of snow. A tongue of it reached out into the path of the traffic. I tried to avoid it, as I might swerve to avoid any living thing, but the tongue had stretched too far. The wheels of the car made a thunk as they passed over it. I had somehow expected the drift to be soft and yielding, like a gathering of newfallen snow. I had not thought of the earth in terms of this hardness.

At the farm I found the sharecropper gaunt of face and in meek voice. There was a dullness in his sound that belied the hope he was mouthing. The grass in the farmyard lawn was brown and ragged with weeds. The house seemed to have shrunk, and its paint was peeling. The apples in the orchard were small and hard. The pasture had been taken over by bull thistles and clattering grasshoppers. The noise of them was conspicuous amid the silence of everything else, and the silence, on the whole, seemed preferable.

I visited the schoolhouse where I had gone as a green youth. There was nothing there anymore. The schoolhouse had been torn down and hauled away. The pump was gone. The swings were gone. The softball diamond was gone. There was in its place a cornfield, and all the corn in it was dead and dying.

I went on to the church of my youth. The church still stood, obscured now by a lean-to vestibule, but the parsonage was boarded up and the shade trees in the little grove to the east of the church were so sparse of leaf that they no longer kept the shade. I wondered how long it had been since children had played tag beneath those limbs or shinned up them in Sunday overalls.

At the back of the church was a little cemetery. The Memorial Day flowers still showed in it. They were all plastic. The graves of my parents are there. I went to them and stood at attention. While I was standing there, tears began to run from my eyes. I did not know what I was weeping for. My tears at least were a kind of benediction: something wet in the midst of all that thirst.

5

In mid-July it finally rained again, and after that the rains kept coming. The Compass Prairie, a tiny island of diversity in a vast sea of uniformity, broke again into brilliant blossom.

There was no tended garden anywhere in the region that was the equal of it: no amount of weeding and watering and fertilizing, no amount of nurturing could create again the equal of the beauty that had been fashioned on the Compass Prairie through a hundred centuries of undistracted experiment.

For three years in a row, the little prairie had been burned in the spring, and each burning had brought the place a little closer to its exquisite state. The weeds that our ancestors carried accidentally in seed sacks from Europe were finally in retreat. Native seeds had sprung up after long dormancies. The eternal grasses had taken hold and spread. Finally in this third year of its grace, there was in that place the picture that the prairie painter Harvey Dunn had once painted and given the title "The Prairie is my Garden."

I went out on the Compass Prairie in the hour of its summer glory and wandered. It was after supper. The farm machinery had quit, and the birds had come out behind the heat of the high day to sing the sun down. It was the hour of the day when the rays of the cool sunshine are longest. They cast upon everything a soft blue haze, intensify all the best colors, and shroud everything in a halo of backlight. The rays of the sun salute everything with tall shadows.

A million insects of every exotic shape and color seemed to be singing a million songs. O. E. Rolvaag, the chronicler of the settlement of the prairies, remarked in *Giants in the Earth* that the prairie was silent when our immigrant fathers and mothers came because there were no insects then. How, I wondered, could a man as careful about the truth as Rolvaag have come to such an astonishing belief?

Many monarch butterflies darted among the blooming milkweeds. There were common milkweeds and swamp milkweeds and whorled milkweeds, all drooping great masses of delicate blossoms and giving off an aroma that filled the summer air as powerfully and as sweetly as the lilacs of urban spring. If we weren't so accustomed to scorning the milkweed, we would bottle its aroma and market it to Paris and make a fortune.

Everywhere there were the lovely drooping blossoms of the cone-flowers, both purple and gray-headed (actually yellow). They were scattered by the hundreds, by the thousands all across the hillside. They were like the daffodils of Wordsworth's England: "Ten thousand saw I at a glance / tossing their heads in sprightly dance."

There were the purple plumes of the leadplants, the graceful white spires of the Culvers root, the golden heads of the black-eyed Susans and the Maximilian's sunflowers.

In all there were more than thirty kinds of flowers showing at once:

> spring stragglers: a rose or two, Canada anemones, water hemlock, downy phlox;
>
> the first goldenrods, each with its aphid-induced gall;
>
> early grasses: big bluestem, cordgrass (the grass that the pioneers twisted into firewood);
>
> herbs: wild mint, prairie sage, wild bergamot, also called horsemint;
>
> clovers: purple prairie, white prairie, sweet, yellow;
>
> Canada milk vetch, daisy fleabane, boltonia, yarrow;
>
> the compass plant, for which the prairie was named, and another yellow flower, the ox-eye;
>
> plants with beautiful names: evening primrose, silver-leaved psoralea.

They were all there, in masses, in waves, a living canvas.

Evening began to fall. The mosquitoes began to swarm and snarl. The crickets started. The moon came up, full and pink, the color of salmon.

In the low places, fireflies began to flash. The homely brown beetles became again marvels, mysteries, the creatures of the night that have made life, as J. Henry Fabre remarked, "one great orgy of light."

The lights were the work of chemistry and the business of females. Sex. So it was with the flowers. Nothing more. So much for wild gardens and nighttime mysteries. It was all part and parcel of the simple ceaseless will in things to survive.

6

I do not keep an impeccable lawn, in part out of slothfulness, no doubt, but also because of a philosophical disregard for lawns.

I cannot fully appreciate the challenge in a lawn: to force nature, by dint of prodigious quantities of labor, of water, of gasoline, of chemicals, to be the one thing it would never be on its own: monotonous. So it happened that my yard in late July was a social embarrassment.

There were dandelions and goatsbeard in the grass, phlox and columbine in the raspberry patch, sow thistles and bellflowers among the daisies. Catnip bloomed beneath the oak tree, which had begun to drop green acorns, and beneath the walnut tree, which had begun to rain green walnuts. There were immense milkweeds among the junipers. The cracks between the patio blocks were decorated here and there with tall hollyhocks, and there was a Scotch thistle of regal bearing at the end of the waterspout.

It was all unspeakably seedy and wonderful.

Once there weren't any weeds here. Once humans didn't know what weeds were, hadn't ever made a name for them. What was, was, and had its place. Where there were roses, roses were meant to be, and where buffalo grass grew, there buffalo grass was meant to grow.

The system survived for a thousand centuries through drought, through flood, through scorching summers, through fierce winters, through the ravages of hail and fire, and it provided food and shelter sufficient to sustain the humans who also lived on the prairie.

When the first white man arrived, there were as many elk and bison and antelope on the prairies as there are now cattle in all the United States. These creatures existed without benefit of tending, tractors, pesticides, barns, loans from the banks, without reference to the rise and fall of the world commodity markets, unmedicated, in a universe where nothing grew except a lot of, as we might say, weeds. Where there was not a straight row of anything to be seen from one horizon to the next horizon. It was a reasonably efficient arrangement.

Weeds: the volunteers in the places where nothing else will grow, the pioneers standing guard against scorched and eroded earth. The edible plants. The plants bearing medicines and potions, teas and seasonings. The splashes of color on the wide landscape. The models of persistence and stamina. The sustainers, against increasing odds, of such wild creatures as remain. The memories, in their genes, of our distant history. The models for all the plants that now thrive in long rows on the grasslands.

I thought about weeds and then went out into my weedy yard one steamy night in midsummer, observing a moment of respectful silence for the remarkable objects of my disgrace.

If I had had a visitor, I might even have offered a toast to my weeds, but it was, lucky for me, a quiet evening, and nobody found me out.

7

I went south to the place where the Platte River joins the Missouri and set up camp there beneath the towering cottonwood trees. The shimmering song of the cicadas sang me to sleep. The dawn came in a subdued dress of gray. Clothed in it, I slipped through the line of cottonwoods and out onto the wide bed of the Platte. I went with empty hands and naked feet.

The Platte is one of the great prairie rivers, or was before it was dammed and diverted nearly to death. It carries between its broad banks the soul of the North American grasslands. It is the river a mile wide and an inch deep. To say that it is a mile wide is scarcely an exaggeration, but to describe it as an inch deep is. In late summer you can hike down much of the middle of it without getting your feet wet. It was so that morning as I set out across it in the lee of a summer storm.

The prairie has struck everybody as a kind of sea. If it is a sea, the Platte River is its beach. The waterways of the prairie, its creeks and flat-banked streams, its ponds and marshes, the wallows the bison made, the shallow, green lakes, are covered with the same immensely fertile black soil that lies beneath the thick sod itself. Where there is water on the prairie, there is mud, thick and deep and rank with the stench of rotting organisms, teeming with trillions and zillions of creatures beyond range of the human eye, organized into communities of a complexity beyond the limits of imagination. The Platte is the island of sand in this labyrinth of mud. It is the shore that bounds the waves of grass.

I walked out onto the river's sandy bottom and down one of its several channels toward the main bed. The fine sand was damp and cool against my feet and particles of it bunched in the spaces between my toes. The marks of other recent visitors—of the pair of jeeps that had been mired in the sand the evening before, of a dog, of a deer, of raccoons and rabbits, of the shorebirds that had been catching shiners in a stagnant pool of water—all of these traces of visitation remained for a while longer on the bottom, but they had been softened by the night's fall of rain. The slate was being wiped clean for another moment in the river's history. With every dawn, every place on earth is a new place. On the Platte, the change is perceptible from one dawn to the next.

The path down the river ran across many drifts of sand, some a few inches, some many feet high. It was a path through little valleys, across wide, flat expanses of tan sands, along snaky rivulets. It ran past puddles, blue-green remnants of the river, which had writhed and churned, boiled even, with the gyrations of hundreds of tiny fish living out their summer days in the faint hope of a flood. Around the rims of these puddles, the carcasses of the fish that had waited in vain lay strewn like silver pebbles.

In the places where the river had run quickest in springtime, the sand gave way to flats of gravel, fine enough to be prickly underfoot but not unpleasant to walk across. There were other things the river had carried with it on its plunge from the grassy sea to the salty sea: the trunks of trees, many small roots and branches polished white as bones, beer bottles and pop cans, dozens of discarded disposable baby diapers, red fragments of barn siding. Of the human artifacts, there were more diapers than anything else. If the holocaust were to descend upon us today, leaving behind the flotsam of the Platte as the record of our civilization, it would be surmised that we were a nation of infants, or of dwarfs who dressed in plastic pants, rendered incontinent, perhaps, by an overconsumption of beer.

The channel I followed was rimmed on the south by a mature stand of lofty cottonwoods, in the shade of which prospered plums and the vines of many grapes. Where the sun could peek through, the floor of the line of forest was bejeweled with little garlands of woodland flowers. Along the island, the channel was decorated with the greenery of succession. Cockleburs had invaded the sand flats and beyond them, on higher ground, grew a thicket of young willows and tall sunflowers in young bloom and beyond the willows in the highest places, there were young cottonwoods: a line of dark green, then of yellow-green, then of silver-green.

Our language does not distinguish green from green. It is one of the ways in which we have declared ourselves to be apart from nature. In nature, there is nothing so impoverished of distinction as simply the color green. There are greens as there are grains of sand, an infinitude of shades and gradations of shades, of intensities and brilliancies. Even one green is not the same green. There is the green of dawn, of high noon, of dusk. There is the green of young life, of maturity, of old age. There is the green of new rain and of long drought. There is the green of vigor, the green of sickness, the green of death. One could devote one's life to a study of the distinctions in the color green and not yet have learned all there is to know. There is a language in it, a poetry, a music. We have not stopped long enough to hear it.

The palette of greens along the Platte speaks also to the perpetual war being waged between the river and the plants that crowd its banks and spring up upon its islands. It is a struggle for dominion over the landscape. The advantage is forever shifting. In the spring thaws and when the rains fall abundantly upon the earth, the river has the advantage, and it has also the armor of its swift running. It has the strength of superior weaponry. In the slack of summer and in times of drought, the community of plants has the advantage, and it also has the force of its relentless persistence. The river ebbs and flows, but the plants restlessly scatter their seeds and send out their shoots, and are always on the march. They have the advantage of superior numbers.

I arrived at a time in the battle when the plants were winning. The platoons of cockleburs were already at the front, and the willows, and behind them the cottonwoods, the brigades of heavy artillery, were not far behind.

I soon left the channel and came out upon the main bed of the river. A sandpiper was feeding there at a pool of water. It caught sight of me, gave a sharp cry, took flight, and landed a hundred yards down-river. I followed it. When I drew near, it flew a little farther. It seemed to be beckoning me to come along. I went where it led me down an expanse of sand so wide that it looked more like the dry bed of a long lake than of a river.

We had not gone far, the sandpiper and I, when the clouds broke and the sun came shining down upon us and upon the glistening sands. Except for the sounds of the bird and of my feet, it was utterly quiet. We were beyond the chatter of the shoreline; the air was warm and still; and it was too early on a Sunday morning for the clank and whine of humans making fun on their machines. The light shimmered. It was a place then as soft as the pinfeather of a young mallard.

I knew that this perception was largely illusory. I knew that the Platte has its quicksands; that when it is running full, it is exceedingly swift and dangerous; that in the world before prairie bridges and Corps of Engineers dams, it was almost impossible to cross in springtime either by wagon or by boat; that its clear and apparently innocent waters are, or once were, a cesspool of infectious organisms; that the line of greenery along the shore is a recent amenity; that the first white man who saw it saw a desolate river passing through a land of desolation.

I knew the river's place in the history of the westward movement. I knew that when one traveled little more than a century ago out of St. Joseph, Missouri, along the Oregon Trail toward the Promised Land, one came inevitably to the Platte River; I knew that the Platte marked the beginning of the long night's journey through the wilderness and that beyond it lay a region of snakes and lizards and prickly pears and little else.

It seemed, to those who crossed it, a place so stark and barren and forbidding that the first adventurers who passed through it could describe it only in terms of ancient mythologies or of other worlds.

Beyond the Platte to the northwest lay the place called by some the Mountains of the Moon. To the southwest of the Platte was a region even more forbidding, the place of the Nebraska salt flats, which the Brule Sioux described, Mari Sandoz reports in *Love Song to the Plains*, as a "region dark with stinking carcasses—buffalo, deer and elk, the stench and silence so frightening that with all of the carrion around there was not a wolf, or coyote, not even a magpie." The reputation of the Platte was such that in 1867 a group of General Custer's own troops died at his order when they tried to desert rather than cross the river.

I knew that the sands of the Platte were once strewn not with disposable diapers but with the scraps of Old Country heirlooms— oaken claw-toothed furniture, legs and bits of hand-carved oaken bureaus and the like—the last home-ties of lonely settlers who had not counted the formidable Platte among the obstacles along the way west. I knew that when thirsty travelers came upon the sands of the barren Platte in mid-summer and dug into them like the bison for the water and drank it, they got relief—and typhoid fever, too.

I knew all that. But I was at the Platte on an enchanted August morning in the company of an accommodating sandpiper; the world was freshly washed; and the river was docile and welcoming.

I walked down the center of it for a mile or two, drinking in its delicious Sunday silence, until I came to a place where the cutting edge of the river had been shored up with the rusting carcasses of dozens of crushed automobiles. It was as if somebody had been painting moustaches on the ancient icons in the sanctuary. I turned back.

Along the way, I happened upon a fisherman who was returning to camp. He had a fish on his stringer; I couldn't see from the distance what kind it was. He was in the center of the narrow stream of the river that still flowed, and he was splashing his way up the current, dip-

ping now and then to give his catch a drink, with such pleasing abandon that I myself was moved to plunge in.

The water was shallow—it scarcely covered my ankle bones in
most places—and it was cool and uncannily swift. The sands on the
bottom glimmered in the refracted morning light. They had been scalloped by the current into an unending pattern of fish scales, and they
were silken and slippery. I splashed my way upstream with greater and
greater abandon. The wily river had conquered me. It had seized me
and sent me spinning down into the hidden part of myself where the
child still lives.

By and by, I had splashed my way back to a place where the bed
of the river splits and goes two ways. I stopped there and turned back
toward the widest expanse of sand and gazed at it again from the perspective of the waters of the river. I thought that I had found the child
in the river too. I thought I could see the time millennia ago when the
waters of the great glacial seas had just receded, when the river was
young and cold and lay naked upon a naked land, when it was waiting,
bright with promise, to be dressed in the green waters of the warm and
grassy sea.

8

There is only one thing they cannot do in flight, and that
is rest.

—Carl Wesenberg-Lund
Quoted in *Insects in Flight*
by Werner Nachtigall

The dragonflies reigned over the prairie marsh in high summer. They
seemed to be everywhere at once, directly overhead, at the water's
surface, among the cattails, out on the open marsh. They could always be found there sailing up and down, back and forth at dizzying
speed but without any apparent effort. They had, in measure as full as
any creature, the quality of grace, the capacity to seem completely at
home in every movement of their lives. The joyfulness of their manner

communicated itself to such creatures, myself among them, as shared in their existence, however vicariously. The dragonflies were joyful not in the sense that they were hilarious, or amusing or diverting, but in a spiritual sense: they had made an accommodation with the world a very long time ago, and this accommodation had worked out; they had achieved a place in the world, and they were suited by design and character to that place, and they were destined so long as that place should exist to have a part in it.

Nature was demanding about place. Every ecosystem operated according to certain constants, and among these was the principle of the sanctity of place. An ecosystem was a system: it had structure and function. Its structure was the arrangement of the varieties of life into mutually exclusive but complementary places. Its function was to sustain life.

An ecosystem was like a mansion with many rooms. The bigger the mansion, the more rooms there were, and the more rooms, the more guests. But there could be only one family of guests per room. Depending upon the demands of the family and the size of its individual members, there might be many individuals in a given room or only a few, but however many or few, the guests in any single room were always all of the same family. If more than one family tried to occupy the same room, there would be a struggle, and the losers would be forced out.

Just as there could be only one family per room, so there could be no more than one room per family. The size of the room put a limit on the population of the family that lived in it. When the room filled up, that was it. The surplus members of the family died.

The number of rooms in the mansion rarely changed, but there was no requirement that every room should be occupied. Sometimes there were vacancies. When conditions were highly abnormal, there might be a great many vacancies. But vacancies were costly: the whole house had to be maintained no matter how many of its rooms were in use, at a constant expense of energy. The more occupied rooms, the more efficient it was to run each of them. So the tendency was always toward a full house.

The room that the dragonfly occupied in the mansion of the marsh had a floor of muck ripe with the smell of decay and a fill of murky water varying in depth from a few inches to two and a half feet, depending upon the season of the year and the conditions of the weather. The air above the marsh was shared by a variety of emergent water plants; vast quantities of the dust of earth and space; birds of many kinds—spring and fall migrants, summering ducks, yellow-headed and red-winged blackbirds, bitterns, gulls, marsh wrens; and vast armies of flying insects—mosquitoes and gnats, flies and wasps, butterflies and moths, cousin damselflies and dragonflies.

There was a thin line between these two zones of water and air in the dragonfly's chambers. It was a line the dragonfly passed through on its way out of the water but did not actually occupy. There were other rooms in the mansion for the holders of this thin film of space, the membrane of viscosity with which the waters of the marsh were sealed. Hydras dangled themselves from this membrane; water striders marched across it; one-celled creatures were suspended within it; and duckweeds floated upon it. But the viscous world was only a boundary in the world of the dragonfly.

The room the dragonfly occupied was very old. The dragonfly was one of the ancient insects, a rare survivor from the steamy jungles of 300 million years ago. It had done remarkably little remodeling in all the ages that had passed since then. The dragonfly that ranged the vegetal swamps of Pennsylvania in that primeval time before the first reptile, the first bird, the first mammal, the first flower, that dragonfly looked very much like the one that hovered today over the waters of the prairie marsh. The first dragonfly, however, was considerably larger. Dragon-flies inspire flights of enthusiasm: one authority says that some early species had wing spans of fifty centimeters, another that the spans extended to seventy centimeters, a third that the stretch of their wings was like that of a great horned owl.

It was a fantastic world then. In the ancient swamps of the first dragonflies, horsetails grew as big as trees. Little horsetails could be found even today at the edge of the prairie marsh. They were, particularly in the springtime before they got the feathery branchlets for which they were named, wonderfully primitive-looking things: simple slender stalks of green, bamboo-jointed, thrusting up out of the earth like asparaguses, offering their spores in little cones, a strategy for reproduction which predated the alluring ways of flowers.

There were older insects than dragonflies: primitive cockroaches, grasshoppers, locusts, crickets. In its larval stage, the dragonfly still retained the ferocious look of its ancestors, the singers in the grass. Perhaps that look had inspired the myth that the dragonfly had a long stinger, a darning needle, which it used to sew shut the ears and mouths of little boys, particularly little Iowa boys, who had been bad. It supposedly came at night and did this sewing, and perhaps it was the connection with the night that had inspired the story that the dragonfly was either a killer of snakes or a snake doctor, in any case something allied with the forces of evil that the snake represented. It was hard to imagine the graceful creature of the daytime air as doing the devil's business, but who could say what went on in the terrifying secrecies of the night?

There were older insects than the dragonfly, but none of these had wings. The dragonfly introduced flight to the earth, and all the fancies that have followed from it. There were dragonflies long before there were humans, and they could already do what humans can't do even now. In dragonflies we have the beginnings of one of our deepest envies.

Dragonflies and horsetails are like the generations of electronic machines that we have come to know, each new model more complicated than the last, more sophisticated, more efficient, less costly to produce, each new model smaller than the last. So it is with the inventions of nature. The trend is toward reductions in scale and magnifications in complexity. We take it as an article of cultural faith that to simplify a thing is to improve it, to make it more efficient, to heighten its artfulness. We celebrate common sense and clarity. But the experience of our own engineering, as of the earth's, is that a system tends to become more efficient as it becomes more complex.

Because the dragonfly is an insect, it achieves adulthood through metamorphosis. Because it is a primitive insect, its metamorphosis is simple and it looks in its larval stage quite recognizably like itself in maturity. In younger and more complicated insects, the process of change might extend through several stages, and at each stage the immature creature might look radically unlike the adult.

The dragonfly began its life in the spectacular tandem flight of its parents over the marsh. When they were soaring through midair, the male fertilized the eggs the female was carrying. They withdrew from their embrace and the female descended, skimmed the surface of the water, dipped the tail of her abdomen repeatedly into it, deposited her eggs, and, never missing a beat of her wings, rose again toward the male who was waiting for her. The delivery of the eggs to the nursery of the marsh waters was a dangerous episode in the mother's life. She was vulnerable then as she seldom was to the jaws of a fish or of a turtle lurking just out of view.

The eggs dropped to the bottom and hatched there. Some of the nymphs were seized by diving beetles and eaten, but a few of them survived and grew to full size and became ferocious predators in the violent world on the floor of the marsh. The dragonfly larva had a double-hinged lower lip which was armed with a pair of sharp, movable hooks. It burrowed itself into the soft mud at the bottom of the marsh and lay in disguise there until some other insect or small fish or tadpole passed within its reach. When one did, it threw out its lip at it and impaled it on its hooks. The position of the hooks was such that the victim was conveniently laid upon the table of the dragonfly larva's mouth. Its powerful jaws then went to work at their leisure.

The larva had a set of gills in its anus through which it breathed by sucking in water, extracting the oxygen from it, and expelling the wastes. It had a full set of legs which it used for crawling about in the mud and for climbing up onto the submerged stems of vegetation, but when it wanted to move through the water itself, it propelled itself on the expelling power of its breathing apparatus.

When fall came and the onset of winter was at hand, the dragonfly joined the host of snails and frogs and turtles and worms and other insect larvae in burrowing down below the frost line into the mud. There it assumed a state of torpor and passed the long and inhospitable season in hibernation.

In the springtime, it awakened with the rest of life and resumed the process of its reconstruction into an adult dragonfly. When it had completed this reconstruction, it made its way to the stem of a cattail and crawled up into the air which would be its home for the rest of its days.

It made the transition to life in the air gradually. For the first three days and four nights after it left the bottom of the marsh, the dragonfly rested on the stem of the cattail with its abdomen still immersed in the water so that it could continue to breathe through its gills.

Very early on the morning of the fourth day, it pulled itself out of the water altogether and began the final stage of its journey from water to air. It was almost two hours before dawn. The dragonfly did not know, of course, why it had chosen to make its transformation at this hour, but its genes did. Something in them remembered that when a dragonfly took shape before the voracious birds had awakened, its chances of survival, and so the chances of survival for the species, were multiplied.

It took more than an hour for the dragonfly to emerge from the shell of its former larval self. First the larval skin split along the mid-dorsal line. Then the dragonfly's mirror-smooth thorax, the middle section of its body, emerged. This section of the body supported the wings and contained the skeletal structure to which they and the muscles that powered them were attached.

After the thorax came the head and legs. The head was almost completely covered by two enormous compound eyes with 28,000 ommatidia apiece. Each ommatidium was equipped with its own lens and retina and gave the dragonfly independently some small range of vision. Together they worked to provide it with a sophisticated sense of sight; the dragonfly would do all of its hunting from now on by sight and could distinguish small movements forty feet away. The legs were positioned so that they could serve as a basket in which to trap insects when the dragonfly was on the wing.

When the feet had fully emerged from the larval skin, the dragonfly used them to get a firm hold on a higher piece of the cattail stem. Using this leverage, it dragged its abdomen free. The first faint tinges of the morning sun were beginning to appear as a vague lightening along the rim of the horizon. The first of the birds were beginning to stir. The emerging dragonfly was then as vulnerable to attack as it ever would be. It was a soft and shriveled thing, and its wings were crumpled in upon themselves.

The dragonfly gasped in air. At that moment, it left behind forever the watery world of its immaturity. The breath of air activated the life systems of its new body. Its abdomen inflated and straightened. Blood began to flow into the veins of its wings, and a liquid began to be pumped into the spaces made by the two thin layers of epidermis that were to be the fabric of the wings. As the liquids flowed, the wings filled and unfolded rather as a party blowout does when air is blown into it. This was another critical moment in the dragonfly's life. If one of the wings did not unfold properly, or if the creature slipped and one of the wings got bent or torn, or if it were attacked now and escaped but sustained damage to a wing, there was nothing that could be done about it. The wing could never be uncrumpled again. The wings the dragonfly got in this moment were the wings it would die with, and it would die very soon if they were in any significant way defective.

As soon as the dragonfly's wings were fully extended, the veins fused with the outer membranes and began to stiffen into hard rods. This took about forty-five minutes. The dragonfly waited for it without moving on its cattail stem. By the time the hardening had finished, the first streaks of sunrise color had come into the sky, and the marsh birds were singing in full chorus. The wings were a marvel of structural simplicity; they were durable; and they were remarkably lightweight: their finished membrane was a little less than one ten-thousandth of a millimeter thick. The hardening completed, the dragonfly flexed its flying muscles once or twice and took to the air.

The mechanical means of its flight were as straightforward as one might expect in a thing designed a few hundred million years ago. There were two pairs of wings secured by a pair of horseshoe-shaped double ribs in the thorax. The ribs were anchored in the solid floor-ing of the thorax, and on either side they were connected by a pair of struts, top and bottom, to absorb the longitudinal stresses of flight (the natural tendency was for the wings to pull toward each other). Each of the double ribs was braced at several points, and the whole structure was covered with a thin membrane of fine epidermis. This apparatus was like the wings themselves, lightweight, sturdy, and economical in its use of materials.

Each of the dragonfly's wings was powered and could be moved independently. The power for each wing was supplied by a pair of muscles which operated as levers across a fulcrum. The outer muscle pulled the wing down, and the inner muscle, using the fulcrum as its leverage, pulled the wings up. The work of the muscles was considerably lightened by one of nature's miracles, a substance called resilin. The dragonfly employed it in the construction of its wing hinges. Resilin is a protein with exceedingly long molecules—they are some of the biggest molecules known—which are wedded into an extremely regular net. The result is a structure rather like that of vulcanized rubber but very much more elastic. In the laboratory, a piece of resilin was stretched to three times its normal length and held that way for three months. When it was released, it returned to exactly its original length. Nothing else exists that is even remotely as kinetic-energy efficient (96 percent). The resilin in the dragonfly's wing hinges made its flight system fantastically efficient.

The handicap in the dragonfly's very simple flight apparatus was that it made heavy demands on its equally simple central nervous system. There was nothing automatic about the dragonfly's flight. For each flap of a wing there had to be first a command to engage the outer muscle, then a command to release it, then a command to engage the interior muscle, then a command to release it. For the whole set of wings to flap once, the nervous system had to issue a coordinated set of sixteen separate commands. This took time. Consequently, the dragonfly's wings flapped rather slowly. There were faster insects in the world than the dragonfly. And the demands on the nervous system were tiring. Many insects could sustain flight for longer periods than the dragonfly.

Still, nothing could fly like the dragonfly. The virtue in the simplicity of its flight system was that it was extremely flexible. The dragonfly could use any combination of its wings, and it could switch combinations almost instantaneously. It could glide. It could hover. It could fly backward as well as forward. It could stop in midair, reverse direction in an instant, make sharp turns, suddenly raise or lower altitude. It was the most mobile flying machine in nature.

I spent half an hour one bright summer afternoon trying to catch a dragonfly. I had a net on a long pole, and I had intelligence and time and patience and a willingness to persevere. There was no reason why the dragonfly should elude me.

I approached the task with a suitable sense of humility. I did not intend to make a show of power. I would stand at the edge of the water at a place where there was an opening in the cattails and simply wait until the dragonfly came within suitable distance of my net. There was no reason why it shouldn't. I had been watching from a bit of a distance, and it was clear that the patrol route the dragonfly was on would bring it inevitably within range. The heat of the sun reflecting off the water was, it turned out, quite oppressive, and the whine of the mosquitoes took something of an edge off the charm of the day.

The dragonfly, it developed, had some sort of mission in a part of the marsh that it had hitherto altogether shunned. I watched it through my glasses. Its swivel-necked head was in constant motion, and it seemed with disconcerting frequency to be swiveling in my direction. Oh, there were so many things the dragonfly had to do in that distant and unreachable province of the marsh!

When I finally despaired of the dragonfly and was resolved to give it the kind of pompous snubbing it was dishing out, it returned and executed a dazzling set of acrobatic turns just outside the reach of my net.

Then the dragonfly came in closer, left the water, and flew out across the land and commenced to tease me mercilessly. I was not about to force a challenge. I brought together my fat arms and raised and lowered them as vigorously as it was within my power to do in the direction of the dragonfly's flight, but wherever the net landed, the dragonfly had just been or was quite shortly to be. I went so far as to begin to move my legs about in pursuit of the dragonfly. Actually, I moved them quite energetically, not that I expected it to do any good. Wherever my feet went, there the dragonfly was not. Perhaps I even said a thing or two to that dragonfly.

The dragonfly seemed finally to tire of the whole business. It went down toward the water again and not all that impressively, it might be added. I followed at a tremendous speed. I had my net raised high over my head. I brought it down at a quite cleverly calculated angle. As the long handle of the net descended, so did the brim of my hat. My eyes failed me in the next instant, and before I could calculate a response, I was dripping here and there, roughly from head to foot, in the ripe and aromatic sediments of an August marsh.

The dragonfly, in the meantime, had caught a fresh lunch.

9

The surface of the water in the pond below Silver Lake Fen was covered with a carpet of duckweeds. They were petite round disks, each with five veins and a single little root dangling below. They were a brilliant waxy emerald green—they might have been swatches of pure chlorophyll—and they glistened like the king's dinnerware in the long rays of the late afternoon sun. The duckweeds were completely free floating. Once in a rare time one of them would flower—one species was the world's smallest flowering plant—but in general they reproduced by budding. A daughter would emerge from a pocket on one side of the plant, grow, and be launched. In the meantime, a second offspring would be started on the other side of the little circle. Each disk would produce four or five new plants in a season, each succeeding offspring a little bit smaller in maturity than the last. But when the offspring reproduced, the first offshoot of even the tiniest duckweed would be full-sized again. Nobody has thought of an explanation for this.

The theme of physiological aging and rejuvenation was repeated in the duckweed world by the planarians, the small triangular-headed flatworms with the comical pigmented eyes. They are the creatures that get cut up in biology classes to demonstrate the power of regeneration. If you chop one in half, its tail grows a new head and its head a new tail. But more remarkable than this is how the planarian copes with famine. Faced with a food shortage, it begins to retrogress toward infancy. Its vital parts begin to shrink. Its sexual organs disappear. Its stomach gets smaller. In the extremity of its hunger, it begins to look again like a newborn planarian. If there should in time be a fresh supply of food, the planarian reverses the process. It eats and becomes adult again.

The planarians were not the only creatures attracted by the rafts of duckweed. Hydras browsed among them. Snails laid eggs on them. An ephydrid fly used the Thalluses as nursery chambers. Fish fry and the larvae of many land insects escaped the sweltering heat by gathering in the shaded waters beneath the duckweeds.

As early evening set in, a muskrat cut a path through the pond on its way to its den in the bank of the dam.

The mallard ducklings had already shed their baby down and taken on the lithe and tall-necked look of adolescence. They too cut paths through the carpet of debris on the surface of the stagnant pond, sticking close to the clumps of cattail reeds in shallow water, where they were out of reach of the snapping turtle that had taken their siblings.

The ducklings chattered as they went. Their call was like the cheeping of farmyard chicks, but higher, sharper, more insistent, like the warning bleep of an overloaded computer or of a street-cleaning machine running in reverse.

There was a loud splash. I stood up from my hiding place to see what had caused the noise. The adult ducks shot out of the water in alarm and flew to the lake nearby. The source of the splash had disappeared. When the sound of the leave-taking of the big ducks had died away, the bleep, bleep, bleep of the ducklings came into focus again. I went up into the fen. I came back a couple of hours later at dusk. The ducklings were still bleeping. Perhaps they went on forever.

The twenty-foot high pile of sedge peat at the center of the fen was festooned with the red-brown blossoms of *Phragmites*, the tall shoreline reed that grows around the central rim of the bog and holds its mound in place.

A month earlier, the graceful plumed stems of last year's *Phragmites* growth had held numbers of screaming male red-winged blackbirds, each of them defending a hidden nest from all invaders. Now the black-birds had left the fen and were flocked in a big cottonwood tree, or were cruising the marsh in flocks, making ready for the annual flight south.

The spongy center of the peat mound showed the tracks of a rac-coon and buzzed with the sawing of crickets and swarmed with frogs and toads, but it seemed somehow ominously silent in the absence of its batallion of blackbirds.

Out on the harsh seepage of the fen, the vegetation looked mowed, as always, because it was so short and thin. It took special qualities of adaptability and endurance to live in that cold, constantly damp, extremely alkaline place. The heavy smell of sulphur permeated the air, and the bottom of every pool of stinking water was covered with a ghostly gray marl of precipitated calcium.

Still the place was festooned with flowers: the elegant, five-pointed, blue blossoms of the lovely brook lobelia showed everywhere, and in the higher places, there were the creamy white, pinstriped, tall-stemmed flowers of the Grass-of-Parnassus. Soon they would be joined by the blossoms of a rare gentian.

Even the forbidding pools, which lay like folds on the fat belly of beak-rush and arrow grass, yielded their harvest of bright color: the emerald green of the leopard frogs that rested in them, the satiny green of the algal slime that floated on their surface; the brilliant yel-low flower of a late-blooming bladderwort, a snaky and carnivorous plant that shared space in the pools with the more primitive and gray liverworts.

There was a killdeer, as always, at the western edge of the seepage, which took off with its hysterical cry as I approached.

Frogs leaped into the pools of water and disappeared into the marl at my advance. I grabbed at one of them with my hand. I felt it slip through my fingers, and when I pulled up my hand, it had taken on the stench of the water.

I watched the water clear, and I saw again the snails that prospered there, the bugs walking on the surface of the water, and the beetles and the worms crawling on the bottom of the pool.

The skeleton of a damselfly was floating there. I reached for it. It squirted out of my grasp on the film of water that held it up. I tried again, and again. Finally, I had it. I admired the damselfly's exquisite and quite unutilitarian beauty: the dazzling green of its slender back, the aqua blue of its underside, the luminous point of royal blue on its tail. I admired its enormous and complex eyes and its gossamer wings. I held it between my fingers as I made my way back to the marsh. When I got there, I looked and saw that the tiny creature had fallen somewhere away.

The sun was orange with the smoke of distant fires. Overhead a swallow teased a pair of mating butterflies. The shadows had lengthened. It was the quietest and most wondrous hour of the day.

In the long rays of the last light of that mild August evening, I looked and saw that the chlorophyll had begun to drain from the long stems of the water plants, that a line of brown had begun to form at the waterline of the pond. I noticed that with the sun suddenly down, the air had become unexpectedly cool against my bare arms. On my way home, drops of a chill rain began to spatter against the windshield of my car.

Days later, the seemingly endless rain finally stopped. The air grew crisp and clear after the fall of night.

The chirp of the crickets in the grass slowed, and the prairie took on the timbre of autumn.

One fine morning before dawn, I came out of my house and saw again, at last, a clear sky and the stars in the heavens. I was a prairie person. I felt at ease. I had gotten my sense of distance back.

Autumn

1

One morning it was still dark when I awakened; the predawn singing of the birds had faded away; the voices of the insects had died; and the air had assumed the crispness of fall. The crunch of dry leaves could be heard underfoot. It was somehow as if it had never happened before. The crows were flying in noisy flocks again. The brilliant blue petals of the gentians had dried up and fallen away, leaving behind only the bright flowers of an aster here or there. The first light frost had come.

The belligerent winds had started. One night they whined again in the corner of the house. When the fog came, it seeped into the bone-joints of the prairie dwellers and ached there.

Even as the fruits on the vines in the gardens continued to ripen, the leaves that had sustained them yellowed and fell away. The view from the windows of the prairie houses got a bit wider with the fall of each leaf. People began to notice the pale sunsets again.

It was football time, apple time, harvest time, hunting time, school time. Footsteps quickened. It was exciting to be in transition. It seemed more like the beginning of something than like the end of it.

It was time for colds and viruses, time to dig heavier jackets out of the closets, time to water the new grass, to prepare the bulb beds for planting.

It was time to press leaves between waxed paper, to bring them home and put them in vases, to walk on the opposite side of the street, where the opportunities to hear them crunch seemed better.

It was time to collect the cocoons of moths and the chrysalises of butterflies, time to bring them in to the safekeeping of bug houses. It was time to wonder what wonders they would bring.

It was time to begin planning for Halloween, to begin anticipating Christmas, to begin wishing there was a little snow on the ground, to gather the shells of the acorns with their faces like owls.

It was time to practice alphabets. It was time to walk through the puddles one last time. It was time to cut flowers for mommy one last time. It was the golden time, the time of rosy cheeks. It was the time especially made for children.

2

My guidebook on trees says that the fruit of the wild plum, although succulent, is too sour to be eaten raw. That shows what the people who write guidebooks know. I happened to have the taste of a raw wild plum, the rich, unsullied, apricoty flavor of it, fresh in my mouth.

I had been out on a remnant of a prairie, intent on admiring some of the New England asters that were in bloom then, when I noticed that a shadow had fallen across my path. Looking up, I saw that I was about to become entangled in a thicket of plums. I saw that some of the plums still hung like grapes in green bunches from the trees and that others had turned the color of rose hips and that still others were already soft and purple and had beads of worm wax on their skins, a sure sign of delectability.

Obeying some automatic impulse, I picked one of the ripe plums, brushed off the worm wax, broke the fruit open, swept away the pit and the worm with my little finger, and sucked out the wonderful yellow-orange flesh. I reached up for another of the ripe plums, forgot all about the asters, and settled into memory. There are certain objects, certain smells, certain sensations that are for me indelibly etched in particular time.

Franklin gulls are for me permanently attached to October, and to freshly turned furrows of earth, and to the clean, sharp stirring of the autumn air at sunset.

The smell of new sawdust belongs to November and brings to mind a buzz saw mounted on a tractor and stacks of split wood and the image of missing fingers and a picture of the nine-fingered man who used to come to our farm once a year to sharpen the scissors and knives and to spice the house with the best of the new gossip.

December is the month of shelled corn, of scoop shovels, of forks with hooked tines.

In January, I can smell the newly scraped and stretched skin of a muskrat and I can hear the blades of my skates scraping across the bare ice of a prairie pond.

February is the month of death. I can see a red flag on a new mound of earth in a cemetery, and I can see the face of my father in it.

March is the month of moving. I see packing boxes and empty rooms and a stream of spilled milk running down the slanted floor of our new kitchen.

In April, I hear the crunch of frozen grass, and I see plates of thin ice on water puddles, and I can feel the ice melting in my mouth.

I have the sound of corn checking wire twanging in my ears in May, and I smell the rotten grain in the bottom of the drill and the musty odor of black soybean innoculent.

In June, I have the taste of Vacation Bible School paste in my mouth, and the dark, damp, cool atmosphere of a church basement brushes my bare arms.

July is a strawberry cream soda and a scoop of vanilla ice cream from a paper barrel and a nest of hornets in the snout of the pump at the school picnic.

August is a wad of fresh wheat gluten and the sweet tip of a foxtail stem and the sound of the grasshoppers in the grain wagon and the fiendish pleasure I once found in pulling a grasshopper apart and watching its clear blood run.

And September is for me forever the month of the wild plums. I ate them as a child by the grocery bagful. I hid them under my bed for the moment when I would be hustled ignominiously off to bed, and I fought fiercely with my twin sister over the lickings from the plum jam pot.

But the wild plum thicket along the north edge of my childhood maple grove meant much more to me than a happy stomach. It was under the spiny arms of the plums that I built my first homes away from home. They were little dugouts with slanted roofs of branches, furnished with a fascinating variety of objects from the junk pile.

It was in one of those houses that I conducted my first culinary experiment, a pair of vile leopard frog legs boiled in rainwater in an old coffee can over a daring and miraculously harmless fire.

It was in another of those houses that I began my courtship with words. I would don the eyeglasses I had fashioned from a discarded Scotch tape dispenser so that I would look more distinguished and would make long, eloquent speeches to vast crowds before great banks of microphones. The memory of those microphones was so vivid that when I eventually sat down before real ones every day in the conduct of my professional life, I was still stirred by their wonder and power.

It was to still another of these dugouts that I brought Eila Jean, my first love, for the planning of our wedding. (We were both six.)

In some sense, all the important themes of my life found their first expression beneath the sheltering arms of a thicket of wild plums.

At a certain time of the year—it seems to me that this was also in September—our plum thicket attracted bats, which would swoop down like barn swallows when I and my sister, propelled by our fear, would provoke them. So there was mystery in those plum trees and the remembrance of having faced down fear among them and having survived it.

In the winter, the plum thicket caught a splendid drift of snow in which we made tunnels and forts. One bright January day, my father made an igloo there just like the one in the picture books, and we had a picnic in it. Every time I think of my father, I think in one instant of him singing "Home on the Range" to me as he held me in his arms beside a fire one summer night, and in the next instant, I think of him working his snow miracle on that January day. Then I am reminded (I didn't always know it) how endlessly I loved him.

But the first thing I remembered when I tasted a wild plum again was a whole succession of sunny and eventless September days when school had recessed and I had shed my shoes and put on my old overalls and gone off to the far end of the plum thicket, where I could safely ignore, even if I heard it, my mother calling me home to do some chore. I had settled down in the grass beside the crickets; I had at my side a sweet bag of plums; and I had simply let the sun shine and my fantasies run. Then, if ever, I had known the glorious taste of being only and always alive.

3

On September 23, the sun rose over the Blue Mounds at 7:15, announced first by a wispy strand of pink. When the sun set that evening, the day had been divided equally into lightness and darkness. It was the autumnal equinox.

Long before the light of the first day of fall had broken, I had climbed to a place on top of the Mounds near the former home of novelist Frederick Manfred. There ran one of the mysteries of my world, a stone fence extending 1,250 feet to the eastern edge of the Mounds, and so placed that it pointed exactly to the spot on the horizon at which the sun always rises on the spring and fall equinoxes.

Whether the fence followed its course by design or by accident, no one knew. There were some, however, who believed that it might be prehistoric and that it might have been made to mark the sun.

At 6:00 a.m., the air had the nip of the autumn about to be authenticated. I stumbled in the darkness as I took my place along the fence. To the south the moon hung, a thick crescent, the hulk of its full body barely visible. In the valley below, the lights of Luverne twinkled.

By 6:30, the eastern sky had noticeably brightened. The trucks on Interstate 90 roared and snarled, but otherwise the world was still largely asleep. On the eastern horizon, a band of orange appeared. After that, the sky lightened so quickly, so imperceptibly, that it came as a fresh surprise every time I turned away for an instant and then turned back and saw the new degree of illumination.

At 6:45, a meadowlark sang in the lowlands. It sang its clear, sweet, complicated song only twice and then fell silent, as if it, too, shared the anticipation. By now it was light enough so that the delicate and subtle colors of fall before the hard frost had been washed into the landscape, the faded browns and soft tans and faint greens. It was light enough to see the colors and shapes of the vast landscape, but not so light as to reveal its blemishes. Everything seemed virgin, unspoiled. Even the farmyard lights glittered like stars.

By 7:00, the red, sweet-tasting fruits of the pear cactuses growing among the stones of the fence had come clearly into view, and the rich red and pink of the stones themselves had replaced the orange of the sky, which had faded away. Soon a rim of bright light appeared at the joint of land and sky. The moment seemed at hand. But the rim of light hung on and on. I seemed to be watching the pot that would never boil.

Finally at 7:13, a little finger of pink poked up over the horizon as if to test the day. And then in a great rush, seeming at first a little north of the fence, preceded by a brilliant halo of yellow, the sun sailed into view. It appeared to have a difficult time getting up over the edge of the horizon. At first, it was distended, a horizontal oblong, like an egg falling over the edge of a cup. But in a moment, the sun had freed itself and come into full view.

It beamed straight as an arrow, down the miraculous line of the fence. I stood watching, certain that I was in the company of others who had stood in the same place long ago at the outer edge of human history.

By 7:20 it was all over. The sun had climbed to the height of the birds and had begun its arc southward, out of the line of the fence. I clambered across the face of the Mounds toward coffee and office.

One meaning of the coming of any prairie dawn from the perspective of the human imagination is that the sun finds the prairie horizon an obstacle to be struggled against.

Never being able to cross the rim of the prairie is very like a particular and universal kind of adolescent dream. The dream exists in an infinite number of variations: I am falling over the edge of a cliff, and I fall without ever being able to reach the bottom. I am at the next-to-last step on a staircase, and every time I take the last step, a new one appears above it. I am walking on crutches, take a step forward; they turn out to be too short. I am jumping from a rooftop, and every time I land, I find myself on another rooftop. I am falling into a well, but I never reach bottom. The most obvious thing to be said about this dream is that it is inspired by the terror of not measuring up.

My daughter, when she was younger, would sometimes look up pity-ingly at me when she was engaged in some enormously pleasurable act, like jumping on the bed, and say comfortingly, "Some day, daddy, when you get small, you can do this, too." Little did she know how brief would be the days of her comfort in this condition. Already she had begun the process of sizing herself up against the world. She was taller than Adam but shorter than Matthew. At the dinner table, she was eager to exchange chairs: "You be Laura and I'll be Mommy." Her life was already obsessed with the pursuit of victories: "I beat you up the stairs." "My bath was longer than your bath." "I have eaten more of my popsicle than you have of yours." The moment was soon coming in her life when the yearning for triumph would assume the proportions of a crisis and then she, too, would dream of falling into bottomless wells.

We take the measure of our worth against the environment. Where there are horizons, we stand tall. When we are obscured, particularly by the barriers of our own construction, we fail to measure up. One of the virtues of the prairie is that it is a place in which people are able to measure up.

Perhaps this is true of any landscape immense enough to be out-side the grasp of our imagination. In a hotel in Zurich one morning, a waiter came up to me and said, "You are from America? Maybe you know my friend who lives in Arizona. No? Well, no matter. He keeps writing me to come to America. He keeps telling me what a wonder-fully big place Arizona is." He shook his head. "I don't know. When I go walking in Switzerland, it seems plenty big enough for me."

But the prairie is also a place in which souls regularly wither. The countryside was once dotted with insane asylums, and everybody had an aunt or a nephew who had gone to live in one. Madness was the cancer of the settlement era on the prairie. Either you faced the iso-lated endlessness with a sense of invincibility, or you collapsed under the strain; there was in the immensity of the prairie fuel enough to feed either fire.

The enduring portrait of this prairie madness is O. E. Rolvaag's of Beret Hansa in *Giants in the Earth*. Beret is seized with terror from the first moment of her arrival on the prairie.

> Beret and the child had now got down from the wagon; the other two women hovered around her, drawing her toward the tent. But she hung back for a moment; she wanted to stop and look around.
>
> . . . Was this the place? . . . Here! . . . Could it be possible? . . . She stole a glance at the others, at the half-completed hut, then turned to look more closely at the group standing around her; and suddenly it struck her *that here something was about to go wrong.* . . . How will human beings be able to endure this place? she thought. Why, there isn't even a thing one can *hide behind!* . . . Her sensitive, rather beautiful face was full of blank dismay; she turned away from the door and began to loosen her dress; then her eyes fell on the centre pole with its crosspiece, hung with clothes, and she stood a moment irresolute, gazing at it in startled fright. . . . It looked like the giants she had read about as a child; for a long while she was unable to banish the picture from her mind.

I went once in the winter to the place Rolvaag had in mind when he wrote the book. There is a cemetery there now. The pine trees Per Hansa wanted so badly have grown tall. They sigh all day long in the relentless prairie winds. The place is on high ground, and there is a swell there, where the Indian grave of the novel must have been, which makes it seem even higher. A century has passed since this place was first settled, but even now it is sparsely populated and little enough disturbed so that it is easy to imagine how it once looked.

I could see a moonlit winter night. I could see the whole landscape covered with sparkling snow until it revealed not a single distinguishing feature. I could hear the emptiness and the wolves howling. I could see the tiny hut and Per and Beret sitting in the dim light of the fire and the three children sleeping in the corner. I could see them sitting empty-handed and silent, nothing to say, nothing to do, no place to turn around in, nowhere to rest their eyes, even. I could feel time dragging endlessly on.

Per might go to the barn or sleep the day away or set out on a trip somewhere. But Beret had responsibility for the toddler, and she was pregnant again. For her, there was no escape. In the midst of all this space, she, like so many pioneer women, was imprisoned and in solitary confinement and in a cruelly small cell. Is it any wonder that she began to brood about how she had sinned to deserve this? Is it any wonder that she, like so many other pioneer women, went finally berserk?

The history of my own place is that, for all practical purposes, it had to be settled twice. The earliest pioneers arrived at the far end of one of those periodic droughts that are characteristic of the plains and were driven from their claims by the clouds of Rocky Mountain locusts that swarmed across the land. One could hear them coming in the distance, it was said, sounding like a freight train. Then they were upon you in multitudes so vast that the sun seemed to have been blotted out, and you could discern that the roaring noise they made was not the sound of their wings but the sound of their mouths. The locusts would chew their way across the landscape in some kind of bedeviled frenzy, eating everything in sight: the grass, the corn, the grain in the bin, the handles off the pitchforks, the sills off the windows, even the harnesses off the horses standing in the yard. For five years, from 1874 to 1878, they came, reducing to stubble immense stretches of Montana, the Dakotas, Nebraska, Iowa, Minnesota, even the western reaches of Wisconsin.

In the year 1879, the locusts didn't come again, although their eggs infested every cranny of the landscape. To this day, they have not returned.

For a long time, nobody could explain these events. Hunt as one might in the years immediately following the pestilence of locusts, not a single living specimen could be found. Among scientists, the search went on for decades. Nobody was able to discover a living Rocky Mountain locust. It was like the act of a clever devil, and indeed, many people devoutly believed that prayer alone had finally driven the locusts away.

The experience was the same in other parts of the world. Locusts would suddenly appear, and they would as suddenly disappear; in the years between outbreaks, the most diligent efforts could not discover a trace of them. They had to be somewhere. This devastation had been occurring through all the memory of humankind.

Annie Dillard continues the story in *Pilgrim at Tinker Creek:*

> In 1921, a Russian naturalist named Uravov solved the mystery. Locusts are grasshoppers; they are the same animal. Swarms of locusts are ordinary grasshoppers gone berserk.
>
> If you take ordinary grasshoppers of any of several species from any of a number of the world's dry regions— including the Rocky Mountains—and rear them in glass jars under crowded conditions, they go into the migratory phase. That is, they turn into locusts. They literally and physically change from Jekyll to Hyde before your eyes. They will even change, all alone in their jars, if you stimulate them by a rapid succession of artificial touches. Imperceptibly at first, their wings and wingcovers elongate. Their drab color heightens, then saturates more and more, until it locks at the hysterical locust yellows and pinks. Stripes and dots appear on the wingcovers; these deepen to a glittering black. They lay more eggpods than grasshoppers. They are restless, excitable, voracious. You now have jars full of plague. Under ordinary conditions, inside the laboratory and out in the deserts, the eggs laid by these locusts produce ordinary solitary grasshoppers. Only under special conditions—such as droughts that herd them together in crowds near avail-

able food—do the grasshoppers change. They shun food and shelter and seek only the jostle and clack of their kind. Their ranks swell; the valleys teem. One fine day, they take to the air.

4

On the fingerling rearing pond in Worthington, a muskrat house began to emerge. As the days of late October passed, it rose to a height of nearly five feet.

I heard the sound of ducks floating across the fog-bound water when I walked around the lake to work before dawn. The swell in the migration of the ducks came in the next-to-the last week of October. They still flew in from the north after that, but in numbers that decreased as the number of minutes of daylight shortened every day. The early morning fell ever more darkly silent.

At Whiskey Ditch and along the shores of Lake Okabena, I spooked the lake-dwelling muskrats in my predaylight walks. One morning I came upon a half a dozen of them in formation swimming rapidly toward the mouth of Whiskey Ditch. They were backlit by a streetlamp, and their shiny backs above the black water made sleek torpedoes. My presence alarmed them. They simultaneously submerged like a flotilla of submarines.

Sometimes there were crows in the morning, and sometimes not. When there were crows, it seemed like spring. When they were silent, it seemed like winter. There were owls too. Sometimes I heard one on my way to work. And hawks.

I went one gray and windy morning in late October to the petroglyphs near Jeffers. The gate to the place was shut tight, and a sign said it would not be open again until spring. The rocks and their mysterious messages from the past had taken the damp winds all to themselves.

Then at the very top of a tree just outside the high wire that fences in the tiny remnant of prairie, I saw a red-tailed hawk. It was watching for mice in the grass below. After a delay that seemed disdainful, it rose from its perch and flew westward to a more private place.

The bird seemed, despite its great size, to dance on the currents of the air, to flutter up and away to its new perch like a bit of cottonwood fluff floating down to earth.

I got into my car and drove toward home. There was still a little green in the grasses, and the dry tops of the fall grasses genuflected in the wind. The leaves had fallen away from the trees so that they revealed their exquisite skeletons. There were geese along the way in a little marsh, arching their necks in their aristocratic manner. The lines of the landscape were soft with the haze in the air, and the landscape was bright with a hundred hues of brown and tan and black.

I was so carried away with the scene that I got lost. No matter where I steered my car, it ended up in Brown County.

In early November, the harvest was running. It was a week or two behind schedule because of the persistent rains and snows of October, but it was bountiful beyond any previous measure, and the days in which it was undertaken were as clear and gentle, as golden with the glow of Indian summer, as any I had ever remembered.

Then came mornings toward the middle of November when farmers working their fields could see in the crisp, clear light of dawn the full moon going down behind them and the sun coming up ahead of them, both heavenly bodies in perfect alignment. It was, like the harvest, a sign of the continuity in things. The sun and the moon, in coming and going together, affirmed a truth of the harvest, which is that every beginning is the child of some ending.

There were people who wanted to cling to the past. They were the people who hadn't looked much at the world outside their windows. In nature, to refuse the opportunity the moment brings is to be extinguished.

The harvest had once been an important part of life. It was once an important part of my own life. It was the time:

Of canning days, of the family becoming a factory line; Dad picking, Grandpa and the children shelling or stringing, Grandma packing, Mom processing.

Of the sweet aroma of newly dug potatoes in fifty-pound gunny sacks.

Of kicking corn down the slippery wagon box, through the endgate which Grandpa regulated, and into the elevator.

Of coming into the farmyard after dark on an autumn night and feeling the frosty air against my cheeks and finding myself warmed simply by the sight of the yellow yard light.

Of the rats that scampered out of the corncribs at shelling time.

Of the cat that went accidently through the combine one day and came out the straw spreader in a hundred pieces.

Of finding dust in the cracks between my teeth after a day of chopping corn stalks.

Of boiling traps in bluing solution over an open fire.

I remember the peace that came at the end of every harvest, however meager, the understanding so rare in human affairs that here was a thing irreversibly concluded, a thing done, over with, past worry.

I went out again briefly at this harvest, mounted a giant combine completely beyond my experience, steered it briefly down the rows of corn at the terrifying speed of three miles per hour, letting the dust and chaff settle again for a few minutes in my hair.

I remembered again that warm sensation of peace which I had nearly forgotten. I remembered again that there is a time for all things and that among them is that wonderful time when even good things come to an end.

5

It was a world almost without a feature; an empty sky, an empty earth; front and back, the line of the railroad stretched from horizon to horizon, like a cue across a billiard-board; on either hand the green plain ran till it touched the skirts of heaven.

—Robert Louis Stevenson
Across the Plains

The leaf of the cottonwood tree wilted, and its store of nutrients drained into the tree's main trunk. The leaf, deprived of its chlorophyll, revealed its fundamental yellow. It was necessary for the leaf to die. Winter was coming, and if the tree could not somehow shed it, the leaf would go on transpiring water in a season when water was some-times in critically short supply. After the leaf had wilted, a separation line formed at its base. The leaf broke off at that line and blew away in the autumn wind. The tree closed the small wound in its branch with a cement of lignified tissue and cork. From then on, the scar where the leaf had been would always show, and never again would another leaf grow in that particular place.

Passing the next day in the vicinity of the tree, I saw the dried and shriveled leaf and picked it up. I saw that it was folded along its spine and that its long outer edges had spiraled in upon themselves. The leaf, even in this terminal stage of its existence, made a handsome show. This had nothing to do with the leaf. Its form was a matter of physiological necessity; whenever a thing taking shape is longer on the outside than on the inside, it spirals.

There are spirals on a grand scale. Whirlpools and eddies are spi-rals. Great storms—hurricanes, cyclones, tornadoes—move in spirals. Our galaxy is in the shape of a spiral. It may be that the universe itself takes the form of a spiral.

There are spirals on an infinitesimal scale. The basic building blocks of life, the amino acids, the proteins, the sugars, are spirals. The genetic codes are written in spirals. The subflooring materials of our bodies—such things as alpha helixes and collagen fibers—are spirals.

To come upon a spiral is to come upon evidence of growth. There cannot be spirals without growth. To come upon a sign of growth is to come upon the fact of life. There cannot be life without growth. Where a spiral exists, there also has a life gone.

It is true in general that the form of a spiral is alien to inorganic things. Any natural object that spirals can be said by definition to be organic. But there are cyclones and whirlpools and galaxies: perhaps the only exceptions, but still exceptions to the rule. Whereas other spirals have growth in common, cyclones, whirlpools, and galaxies are all phenomena that exist only in turbulences.

So it can be said that where there is a spiral there has been either life or turbulence. Perhaps this is not so much of a distinction after all.

I got into an airplane and flew south across Minnesota, Iowa, northern Missouri. The lakes were covered with ice at this time of the year, but there was no snow on the ground. The crops in the fields had lately been harvested, but it had been a wet and difficult fall, so little plowing had been done. The occasional strip of land that had been plowed was an accent mark on a landscape that was, from 5,000 feet up, a study in browns and grays.

Whenever I went up in an airplane, I thought again of the image I had once read somewhere of an imaginary flight over the nighttime prairie a century and a half or two centuries ago. Imagine, the writer had said, that there had been a prairie fire during the day; that it had swept across hundreds of square miles of the grasslands, as such a fire might well have; and that it had burned itself out by nightfall. What one would then have seen by the light of the moon, the writer said, was a vast expanse of blackness, of landscape without an identifiable feature, except that scattered all across it like thousands of distant stars would have been the glowing embers of the buffalo pies burning themselves out.

At nighttime even now the prairie landscape had from the air a starlit quality, the product of the thousands of farmyard lights that sparkled all across it. But there were many fewer lights now than there had been in the days before people worried about energy shortages, and they did not manage to seem either dreamy or reassuring, as the buffalo pie embers might. They seemed instead to accentuate the isolation in which people lived on the prairie, to give it the appearance of an outpost, to send up an impression of loneliness.

By day the modern prairie landscape was neither ethereal nor especially lonesome. It looked, on the contrary, quite orderly and contemporary.

The lakes took round forms, as all things do when spread across plane surfaces from a center. The streams meandered, as all natural streams do, and branched, as all such living structures—bolts of lightning, branches of trees, blood vessels in a body, veins in a leaf—do. The valleys followed the meanders of the streams that had forged them. The hilltops, to the extent that they could be discerned, took domed shapes which had been further rounded by centuries of wear. It was a landscape innocent of straight edges and square corners.

But it was difficult to pick out the qualities of the natural landscape from the air until one had passed from the grasslands into the region of the Ozark foothills. Not until one reached the foothills did the landscape refuse to yield to the rearrangements of humans. In the foothills, there were the open pits made by the coal miners, remarkable from the air for the brilliance of the green waters that filled them, but even those gashes and the green waters, garish as something baked in plastic, could not obscure the essential character of the countryside.

It was on the open prairies that the prodigious work of humans insisted upon itself as the dominant fact of life. The landscape no longer wandered and wound; it no longer seemed to rise and fall in swells and swales; it no longer stretched around the circumference of the horizon under the great dome of the wide skies.

The rivers in the new landscape were the highways, and they ran straight and true from east to west, against the grain of the continent, from the old world to the new world, from the land of the known to the land of promise, from the given to the mystery, at cross section to the mountains, to the rivers of water, to the skyways, to the paths of the winds. They set in concrete a new order founded not in the nature of matter but in the ground glass of a surveyor's scope.

"Straight is the way and narrow is the gate which leadeth unto life." The believers who gave shape to the new world garden organized it along paradisiacal lines: clean, undeviating, easy to maintain, efficient for establishing boundaries of ownership. Their paths took the high way, even when that sometimes meant running contrary to the lay of the land. Earthly things were *supposed* to frustrate the best expectations of humans.

From the air a century later, one could see the compromises that were being struck. There were the contour strips within the rectangles of farmland, and in some places now there were circles within the rectangles, the tracks of pivotal irrigation systems. On the edges of some prairie towns, one could see now and then a cluster of houses arranged around a cul-de-sac. But the general rule of things was still the straight line, and the rectangle was still the shape to which it was almost always bent.

The prairie people live in rectangular houses on rectangular lots on rectangular blocks in rectangular villages in rectangular counties in rectangular states. To be right with the prairie world, I could see from the air, is for us to be always at some kind of right angle to it.

The language the prairie people speak is as given to straightnesses as the houses they build and the cities they plan and the row-crops they till. Or is it the other way around? Is it the language that started it?

We say that a person who has a clear idea of things is a straight thinker. A person who gives a full and honest account of things is someone from whom you can get a straight answer. A person who is aboveboard in commercial matters is said to be a straight dealer.

To tidy a thing up is to set it straight, to operate without deviation from principle is to be straight, to get a thing right is to get it straight; and it is best if one can be straightforward about such matters and to see to them straightaway.

To be straight is to be respectable, normal, predictable; not given to homosexuality or to the ways of teenagers or to atheistic or Communist thoughts. One can go too far, of course. One can become straightlaced, but that is a far cry from being eccentric, or worse.

What one wants in a man is that he should have his affairs squared away, that he should be one to offer a square deal and a square meal, that he should be square-shouldered and a square shooter, that he should be the sort of person one can look square in the eye.

What, on the other hand, is there to be said for roundness? It suggests plumpness to be sure, a certain shapeliness. But nobody really hopes in the end to be regarded as the round-shouldered type; or as a person round of speech, that is, outspoken; or as a practitioner of circular, that is, false, reasoning; or as a person of circuitous means or as a traveler by circuitous routes; or as a circumventer rather than a doer. Life, after all, is not a circus.

I stood upon a feeding bed at the edge of the marsh. When I tired of watching the migrating pelicans, I turned my attention to the debris at my feet. It was a thick mat of stalks and bulbs, the remains of the abundant harvest to be made among the dense cattails that grew out a hundred yards from the water's edge. Among those reeds was to be found as rich a diversity of life as anywhere on the prairies.

There were in this debris, among other things, many shells; here were the claws of a crayfish, and here were the shells of the pond snails, right-handed, disk, left-handed. I picked up the shell of a disk pond snail and the shell of a right-handed snail and took them home to my study. The shell of the right-handed snail got crushed beneath a book one day when nothing else was going right either, but the disk snail's shell still remains at my side as I work in my windowless cell.

It is a fine, adult specimen, three-quarters of an inch across the coils, three-eighths of an inch wide at its opening, beginning at its core in an off-white and yellowing gradually as it coils around itself until, on the fourth turn, it begins to be almost brown. Its growth, the result of secretions of calcite from the snail's skin as it grew even larger, is recorded on the coils in a series of delicately raised bands. On one of the flattened sides, the coils are evenly raised. On the other, they are recessed, so that they show how the coils broadened in proportion as they grew in circumference.

The disk pond snail did not lead a romantic life. Its was a life spent upon the water plants in muddy-bottomed places rasping up such food as happened by. It had grown slowly, had moved slowly, if at all. It had hosted parasites. It had hidden from its many enemies. It had mated, although it was hermaphroditic. Perhaps it had been a bit of a scavenger. Perhaps not. It was one of those creatures of no known importance to humans. So far as anybody could see, it did no harm, no good. It might have ended its life as food for a predator. Perhaps it simply died. Who cared?

But there is this: a connection exists between the disk pond snail shell on my desk and the scrap of Parthenon marble I also keep there.

It is a connection that has something to do with proportion and grace, with numbers and fancy distinctions. Perhaps it is one of those angels-dancing-on-head-of-a-pin distinctions. Perhaps it is simply an amusement, an accident of no consequence.

Still: there is something known as the golden rectangle, a rectangle with proportions of roughly 5:8. There are those who argue that the shape of the golden rectangle is asethetically superior to rectangles of other proportions; that the proof of this is in the frequency with which such rectangles can be found in the master works of art. Artists no doubt produce golden rectangles unconsciously, the argument runs, but they produce them. The aesthetically focused eye knows instinctively what can also be demonstrated in formal mathematics. Hence, there is, among many other wonderful examples, the facade of the Parthenon, a perfect golden rectangle.

It happens that if one draws within a large golden rectangle a progression of ever smaller golden rectangles, and then draws a cater-cornered arch through each, proceeding in clockwise direction from the lower left-hand corner, one will produce a logarithmic spiral, the most common kind of spiral in a natural world full of spirals. One will produce, in fact, a spiral that exactly describes the shape of the common, the boring, the useless, the inconsequential, the perfectly gorgeous disk pond snail.

6

An Indian hunter on the prairie is like a cruiser on the ocean, perfectly independent of the world, and competent to self-protection and self-maintenance. He can cast himself loose from every one, shape his own course, and take care of his own fortunes.

—Washington Irving
A Tour of the Prairies

In mid-December, a mass of bitterly cold arctic air swept across the prairie. It had been preceded by a heavy shower of fluffy, big-crystaled snow which fell like confectioner's sugar in the great stillness and dusted over every scar in the landscape. Almost nothing moved in the frigid aftermath of the storm.

I went out onto the Blue Mounds on one of those poststorm days when the mercury in the thermometer did not climb past zero. For long stretches of my way, I did not see anything in motion, nor could I see even the tracks of the creatures that had once been in motion.

There were the tracks that the stems of the grasses made when they stirred in the breeze; along the creek still running from a spring, there was a rabbit trail; there had been a deer and a rabbit or two along the edge of the pond; and here and there were the signs that a rodent had surfaced from the labyrinth of tunnels in the sod below. But these tracks were not sufficient in sum to give the impression that the place was any longer occupied.

The whiteness and silence made the prairie seem, despite all the farmsteads visible in the valley below, infinite and unsullied. It had the strange allure of a dream.

The frozen carcass of a pheasant was laid to rest in the fence along the buffalo run. The other pheasants, and the other birds and the mammals, and the reptiles, and the insects, every other living thing had taken shelter somewhere, in one of the draws or underground, or in the lee of one of the rocky cliffs.

But the bison were out grazing on a hillside, using their beards and their massive muzzles to sweep away the loose snow from the curved grasses. They were rooting in the snow, like pigs in the earth, and at long intervals, one or another of them would give out a piglike snort.

Great clouds of steam rose from the bisons' mouths. The frisky calves cavorted. They pestered their mothers which chased them away when they got to be too much of a nuisance.

The bison were splendidly built for the open winter. They wore their sleek, thick coats of dense, fine fur, coats as warm as any in nature, as the Indians, and later the white pioneers, came to appreciate. The bison stood on their short, thick legs, powered by the massive muzzles of their barrel chests, their huge, bearded heads close to the ground.

A bison seen close-up in summer is not a thing of beauty. Its winter fur hangs on in scraggly patches. Cowbirds perch on its back to harvest the abundant crop of ticks and fleas that live there. The animal is constantly swarmed by masses of flies, which it is forever swatting at ineffectively with its ridiculously short tail. It is dirty from wallowing, and its beard hangs in matted clumps.

None of this is so in late fall. The swarms of insects have disappeared; the predator birds have gone; it has grown a luxurious coat. The bison's slow gait across the grasslands seems then not ponderous but regal.

Once upon a time there was a culture in which the bison was worshiped as royalty. It was the Plains Indian culture of the eighteenth and nineteenth centuries. It is worth remembering because there may never have been so intimate a connection between human society and another kind of creature as there was between the Indian and the bison.

The bison, of course, provided the Indians with food. The meat was taken fresh in the summer or after a hunt, beginning with the delicacies eaten still warm at the butchering: livers, kidneys, tongues, eyes, testicles, belly fat, stomachs, leg bone marrow, the hooves of tiny unborn calves, brains. At camp, there would be grilled ribs, soups, blood broths, sausages, udders grilled with the milk still inside, lungs boiled with corn, baked rumps, roasted bones.

Between hunts, there would be smoked tongue, smoked fat of the bison's hump, jerky, pemmican, and in times of destitution, even skins boiled with berries or served plain as a soup or jelly. Except for horns, hooves, and hair, no part of the bison did not in some way figure in the cuisine of the Indians, down to the bile from the gall bladder which was made into a sauce for raw liver.

From the bison came also shelter: tepees and lodges were fashioned from their hides, as were the sweathouses in which the Indians took their constitutionals—these were operated on the same principles as the Finnish saunas. Inside the tepee or lodge, the floor was likely to be of bison hides; there might be partitions of embroidered and decorated hides; and the bed might be a hide stretched over four posts and covered with hide blankets.

From the bison came also clothing of all kinds: robes, shirts, leggings, breechclouts, dresses, hats, moccasins, gloves, the winter garments made from skins with the hair left on, the lighter summer garments from skins that had been denuded.

From the bison came also drink: in times of drought, the contents of the stomach might be swallowed or the gristle of the nose might be chewed; both could quench parched throats. The blood of the bison was drunk and so was the milk.

Food, shelter, clothing, drink: every physical necessity of life came from the sacred bison. But this was only the beginning of its bounties.

From the green hides came knife sheaths, cups, dippers, kettles, mortars, rattles, drumheads, cradles, cages, fencing, snowshoes, boats, packing cases, shields, bridles, ropes, pieces of saddlery, horseshoes, fasteners, clubs and mauls, storage sacks. A tough battle armor could be made from processed hides.

From bison hair came a lining for moccasins; a stuffing for saddles, dolls, balls; a spun wool for blankets, scarves, bags, wallets, women's girdles; braided ropes for halters, lariats, belts, and cords. The women made earrings, bracelets, and garters from bison hair. The Plains men fashioned earrings and hairpieces from the same source.

From bison horns came arrowpoints, drinking cups, powder flasks, trimmings for war bonnets, emblems of high office, spinning tops for boys, instruments for flattening porcupine quill embroidery, heads for war clubs, cupping horns for bleeding patients to relieve infections, spoons, ladles, bows, dinnerware, and firepots. Pieces of horn simmered with spruce needles made an eye medication.

From the bison hooves came spoons and glue.

From the bones of the bison came saddle trees, war clubs, pipes, knives, knife handles, arrowheads, arrow-making tools, runners for dog sleds, spades and hoes, fleshing and graining tools for hide curing, paintbrushes.

Teeth were used for many kinds of decorations.

Bison sinew provided threads and bindings of many kinds.

Bison paunches made water canteens, dried meat wrappers, collapsible buckets, saucepans. Heart and bladder sacs were used for the same purpose.

The bladder could be fitted with a bird-bone nozzle and used as a syringe.

Intestines made bindings and containers.

Toys, musical instruments, cosmetic aids, paints came from various parts of the bison.

Buffalo chips were prized as a fuel: early white settlers joked that steaks cooked over them were so tasty they didn't even need to be peppered. Pulverized, they were used as a tinder for starting wood fires and as an absorbent papoose liner—an early version of the disposable diaper.

If you were born on the plains, you started life swaddled in the soft skin of an infant bison calf and you ended it in the bison-hide coffin that transported you to your grave. The bison was quite literally the beginning and the ending of your existence.

For thousands of years, it seemed as if there could be no end to the bison. The Plains Indians believed they were eternal. They hadn't envisioned us. We arrived upon the Great American Desert, as we called it, in the nineteenth century, determined to conquer it, to make it flower with the fruits of our own labors.

In 1802 the last bison in Ohio died.

In 1832, the last bison in Wisconsin, two of them, were slain. None were ever seen again east of the Mississippi.

In 1833, the great prairie explorer Josiah Gregg warned that if the wanton slaughter of the bison did not stop then, our habits "must ultimately effect their total annihilation from the continent."

"Before many years," John James Audubon warned a decade later, "the Buffalo, like the great Auk, will have disappeared. Surely this should not be permitted."

By 1849, the great overland rush was on. A man named Randolph B. Marcy published a travel guide in that year for people headed west. It was a model of practical information—advice on what to pack and what to leave behind, how to choose good mules and oxen, where to find reliable guides, what routes to take, where the best camping spots along the way were to be found.

By and by, Marcy comes to the subject of the buffalo: "The largest and most useful animal that roams over the prairies is the buffalo," he says.

It provides food, clothing, and shelter to thousands of natives whose means of livelihood depend almost exclusively upon this gigantic monarch of the prairies. Not many years since, they thronged in countless multitudes over all that vast area lying between Mexico and the British possessions, but now their range is confined within very narrow limits, and a few more years will probably witness the extinction of the species.

The odds, Marcy advises, are already very much against encountering a bison in your travels, *but* if you should be so lucky, here's the best method for shooting one, and you ought to know that the rump and the tongue are the choicest cuts for your table, and you really needn't bother about the rest.

It soon became, in an offhand way, government policy to try to exterminate the bison. The Congress passed legislation in 1874 to protect the few bison that remained, but President Grant refused to sign it and it died of a pocket veto. He was following the advice of his secretary of the interior, Columbus Delano, who regarded the extermination of the bison as the final solution to the Indian problem.

The same year, the State of Texas tried to take preservation action on its own, but the day was carried by General Phil Sheridan who rushed to San Antonio to tell a joint session of the Legislature that

instead of stopping the hunters you ought to give them a hearty, unanimous vote of thanks and appropriate a sufficient sum of money to strike and present to each of them a medal of bronze, with a dead buffalo on one side and discouraged Indian on the other. . . . Send them powder and lead if you will, but for the sake of a lasting peace, let them kill, skin and sell until the buffaloes are exterminated. Then your prairies can be covered with speckled cattle and the festive cowboy, who follows the hunter as a second forerunner of an advanced civilization.

In that year, 1874, the last of the southern herds of the bison expired, victims of a three-year rain of professional hunters' bullets which yielded at least four million carcasses for the hide trade. The hunters headed north.

In Texas, the settlers were more frugal than elsewhere: at least some of the bison bodies left behind were turned to use as pig feed. But across the wide prairies, the quantities of rotting carrion gave up a stench that hung over the land. Farmers settling in Nebraska and Kansas in the 1870s sometimes found it necessary to pick the bison bones from their claims before the land was fit to plow.

And then in 1886, William Hornaday of the U.S. National Museum, later to become the Smithsonian, took inventory of his collections and discovered to his dismay that he did not really have good display specimens of bison. So he organized an expedition to Montana to right this deficiency. His party hunted for eighteen days without spotting a specimen. At last they came upon a band of seven bison and managed to kill four of them. The next day they bagged another four. Over the next two months, they managed to find and kill another seventeen animals before returning home.

The year after that, the American Museum of Natural History, feeling the competitive spirit, decided to follow in Hornaday's footsteps. A party from that museum scoured the same Yellowstone-Missouri divide for three months, and in all that time they did not encounter a single bison. They finally gave up and went home empty-handed.

7

The weather vacillated in mid-December between vestigial fall and early winter. For days at a time, it would be gray and frigid, and then a wave of sunshine would suddenly wash in and as suddenly recede.

On one of the sunshiny afternoons, I climbed the cliff of the stone quarry at Blue Mounds. A flight of pigeons roosting on a rocky ledge took off at my approach. Sparrows were singing in the oaks at the foot of the cliff. In the distance, a crow called.

The route up the cliff was through a crevice in the wall where I had seen a weasel a few days earlier. There were only a few patches of snow on the ground, but the weasel was already dressed in its winter coat of white.

Atop the cliff, the patches of snow in the crannies of the rocks had melted into little water puddles. The freshened mosses in the puddles made bright green splotches on the brown landscape of early winter.

Other brilliant snatches of color decorated the high and wind-swept prairie. There were the orange-red hips of the prairie roses and the red fruits of the pear cactuses. Browsers had already cleaned the soft, sweet, jellylike pulp from many of the cactus fruits, leaving behind the shredded skins of the fruits with their tiny, treacherously barbed spines. There were the dazzlingly orange patches of one of the varieties of lichen growing on the pink and maroon outcroppings of Sioux quartzite.

A lichen is a marriage between two plants, an alga and a fungus. The union results in an entirely new species capable of carrying on life under the most inhospitable of circumstances.

On the highest mountaintops, in the coldest and remotest stretches of the arctic and the antarctic, on the hard and ancient surfaces of the Blue Mound rocks, in places where almost nothing else grows, the lichens flourish. The manna that sustained the children of Israel on their journey across the desert was probably the lichen *Lecanora esculenta,* a species that is sometimes driven in great drifts by the winds across the barren sands of northern Africa and Asia Minor.

The relationship of the partners in the lichen marriage is complex and mysterious, but each contributes an essential skill for survival: the alga manufactures food with its chlorophyll, and the fungus captures water from the air; and the two trade these essential commodities as well as, perhaps, certain chemicals.

It is a splendid arrangement, since the algae are generally at home in aquatic environments, and the fungi, which lack chlorophyll, have always had to get along by one kind of mooching or another. Together, the two humble plants have been able to conquer the world.

I knelt on a ridge of exposed bedrock and counted in the space of a square foot at least eight varieties of lichens, distinguishable both by their form and by their color, eight variations on a remarkable and generally unremarked theme.

I passed over the ridge and into a shallow valley. Four white-tailed deer were grazing there among the dry grasses. At my approach, they bounded away into a ravine. Half a mile distant, another group of seven deer were grazing. They, too, disappeared into the cover of the oaks below the ridge, their tails flashing an elegant alarm as they went.

In a little while, they appeared again and resumed their feeding, keeping a wary distance. Their paths took them in an arc around me, the watcher who was also being watched.

The curiosity of one of the deer could not, finally, be contained. He broke from the herd and came forward, ears cocked, eyes intent, every muscle poised for action. He came eventually to within a hundred yards of me, and then we faced off, human and deer, and studied each other. Sound and motion seemed to have been banished.

The deer broke the spell. He took graceful flight suddenly, and with no apparent provocation. At the park boundary, the animal leaped a pasture fence and was gone.

I passed down the valley, scaring up a covey of Hungarian partridges; passed the pond in which the frogs slept; passed the dens of ground squirrels, of gophers and badgers also asleep, of a fox that had left recent tracks; passed among the sleeping seeds, the sleeping insects, the sleeping snakes; passed by the puddles of snow water; passed by the gnarled and active oaks.

I turned over the opened acorns of the oaks and found the cocoons of insects in them.

The shadows lengthened. In the low light, the spines of the tufts of porcupine grass at the edge of the cliff looked like spun silver.

At the quarry, the pigeons circled again, and the sparrows were still singing.

I climbed down the face of the cliff, which would age in the freezing and thawing of another winter. I climbed past the crevice in which the ladybugs slept. I passed by the spider that had spun a bag of silk as armor against the oncoming cold. The moisture on the surfaces of the rocks had begun to freeze, and they were slippery. I climbed down through the edge of another winter.

8

Nature's silence is its one remark, and every flake of the world is a chip off that old and immutable block.

—Annie Dillard
Teaching a Stone to Talk

I went out one night at Christmastime to a party in the country. The day was one of those treasures December brings, half-expected because it is already winter, a day before the first lasting snowfall when the cloudless sky is the color of a blue eye and the rays of the sun melt the surface frost and the birds are singing again after the hiatus of late fall and the air has ceased utterly to move.

The party was planned for dusk. While the children rode upon a barebacked pony, the rest of us set out across the early winter evening on foot. Underfoot, the ground gave way. Where it was bare, the soil came up in clumps on the soles of our shoes. The direct rays of the sun had already disappeared, and without their warmth, the air was fresh against our cheeks. The company took on a blush.

It was the time of day for walking and not talking. The sound of feet against earth passed for conversation. By sound alone, these steps were not distinguishable from the footsteps of any of the other creatures that were given to trod the abandoned road that led to Otter Creek.

It was not yet time for the stars to shine. There was a sunset, but it was not the sunset of paintings or photographs. It amounted to a few streaks of the palest salmon pink against the pearl-gray western sky. Nobody remarked upon it, or ought to have. At this time of day, the branches of the cottonwoods (there were two of them along the fenceline) showed profiles more black than brown. Their ragged and tattered limbs clawed against the last light. These cottonwoods were the end of a line planted a century ago when agriculture was young and when there were still places where prairie could be found. They were refugees in the wide green sea of the grass called corn.

By and by, we came to Otter Creek. There was still open water in it running imperceptibly down from the apparently level track toward the Floyd River, which came eventually to the Missouri, which flowed to the Mississippi, which ran to the sea, carrying with it day by day a few more grains of the dwindling soil that had once laid so thickly upon the earth.

There was no longer anything to Otter Creek. It had once, it is quite possible, sheltered an actual otter. But there hadn't been one for a great many decades. There hadn't been, for that matter, a creek for a great many decades. It had been straightened a long time ago in the days when the tools to do it were steam-powered. An act of mercy took the meanders out of Otter Creek and drained away the marshes through which it ran and scared off or killed the animal life that it had sustained. Otter Creek was now deep and narrow and otterless, a lifeless wound, a barren black rupture in the landscape. It had given its life so that the hungry children of the world might be fed and so that the people who fed them might be freed from the diseases that were thought to be spread by the mosquitoes that multiplied in the swamps and so that fortunes might be accumulated. In 1912 and 1917 and 1923, the prairie marshes seemed filthy things and repugnant to worthwhile human enterprise.

We stood in the waning light of the December day and looked first up and then down the straight, efficient, naked ditch carrying its seasonal pittance of water southwestward and saw nowhere any sign of life or habitation, no bird overhead, no nest or burrow underfoot, no track in the mud, nothing to give credence to the name Otter Creek. And yet, the name remained and had currency. It remained, perhaps as a romantic reference to time past; or perhaps it was meant as a talisman, as a charm holding out hope for life in a time to come; or perhaps it remained as an unspoken prayer: "Father, forgive us for the otter that was, for the creek that ran here, forgive us for forgetting the time when things were more complicated."

When we turned back toward the farmhouse, we saw with surprise that the way was uphill, that we had descended some dozens of feet in the mile we had come. In every direction, it now seemed, there was the inescapable upper rim of the horizon. As always on the prairie, it seemed necessary to climb up to get out. It was a fresh reminder of the essential roundness of the prairie landscape, despite the contrary evidence of our deceptive human eyes.

Our eyes are deceptive because they are trained on the things we find beautiful, and beauty for us is one particular thing in one planned place at one time. It is a lawn, or a cornfield, or a structure with square corners and straight edges, or a note sounded on time and in pitch; some thing that operates according to rules we have devised or can control.

We ask simplicity and order of nature, and it gives us complexity and profusion. We seek to possess it, and it comes to us without a price. We aspire to dominion over it, and, like the star in Robert Frost's poem, it asks of us a certain height.

There is another vision of beauty. It is the one that the boy Black Elk saw in the depths of a fever one night in the dying days of the Sioux nation. His vision is recorded in the book *Black Elk Speaks*.

In his vision, Black Elk saw the four corners of the earth. He saw in the west, the seat of storms, twelve black horses with lightning in their manes and thunder in their nostrils. He saw in the north, the home of the white giant, the seat of the wind, twelve white horses, and overhead white geese soaring and circling. He saw in the east, the seat of the morning and of all singing, twelve sorrel horses wearing elk necklaces, and he saw there the place where the sun always shines. And in the south, the place you are always facing, the seat of happiness, Black Elk saw twelve buckskin horses and he heard the voice of the south which covers all generations.

In his vision, the boy Black Elk also saw the six powers. In the west, he saw a cup of water and a bow, the power of life and the power of destruction. In the north, he saw a white wing, the power of cleansing and endurance, and a sacred herb, the power of healing. In the south, he saw a flowering stick, the power to grow. In the father sky, Black

Elk saw the eagle, the power of protection. And in the mother earth, he saw the sacred tree, the power of renewal and of history. "A man without history is like the wind on the buffalo grass."

He also saw the sacred hoop, the symbol of unity and of eternity, but he saw that there were many hoops, just as everywhere is the center of the world.

Black Elk saw two roads: the black road running from east to west, the road of troubles and wars; and the red road running from north to south, the good road.

And he saw the four ascents:

First, he saw a green land. He saw the sky filled with clouds of baby faces.

Then he saw the babies in the clouds become creatures of the earth. He saw them grow restless. He saw the leaves beginning to fall from the holy tree.

Then he saw the black clouds. He saw the winds of war. "Each one seemed to have his own vision that he followed and his own rules." He saw the nation's hoop begin to break apart like a circle of smoke.

Finally he saw the bison, the source of the nation's strength, disappear. In the place where the sacred tree had been, he saw a sacred herb with blossoms in the four colors of black, white, red, and yellow. From the herb he saw a new tree spring forth.

We say "ashes to ashes and dust to dust," but we don't believe it. We say "in the beginning, is now and ever shall be," but we don't believe it. In our cosmology, there aren't four corners or six powers or four ascents. The earth is not mother to us, and the sky is not our father. We do not see our fortunes in trees or eagles or bison: we do not spring from the earth as they do. In our vision, man came from woman, and woman came from God on a day in creation all her own.

The world Black Elk saw was full of magic circles, of hoops and rings, disconnected every one, but still the same. The four corners of the earth were connected in a circle, and the journey from sky to earth and back again was in a circle, and the vision of the four ascents is a vision of human history that resembles the circle of the seasons. Black Elk sees cultures rising and falling and rising again as things that travel in circles inevitably must. He sees that in any natural life there is ebb as well as flow. His sorrow is that he should have been born in the ebb of his nation; his hope is that it does not matter, that there will be a day when the spirit of his nation springs forth again from the earth and flourishes in the manner of all life. He sees us and our beliefs as similar to the seed that falls from the trees and brings forth a new tree. The new tree is not the old tree, but it is still the same tree.

The pioneer Beret Hansa in *Giants in the Earth* personifies the geometry of our own beliefs. Beret looks out across the vast prairies to the horizon, and she too sees a magical circle, but for her the circle is a vision of terror. She sees it as a trap, a fence which binds her to the earth and from which she will never escape. Her only hope is in death, for which she earnestly and morbidly prepares. Her hope is in death because the geometry of life as we know it runs in a straight line: we are here, and the devil is in the fiery pits below, and God is in the heavens above; and when we die, we will either go up, as on a string to the heavens forever after, or we will fall screaming into the fiery pits below forevermore. For us, there is no cycle in things. Life is all up or down. We are not here on earth because we are of the earth. We are, as we have sung so many times in so many hymns, merely sojourners here, strangers passing on through to the brighter life of the world yet to come.

We may be diverted by what is strange to us for its exotic qualities. The glory of the sunset or the spectacle of the leaves in fall color or the mystery of a bird or butterfly in flight may arrest us for this reason. But that is not the same as being in love with nature. We ultimately commune only with others of our own faith, and for us westerners, nature is an article out of another faith. The road we travel is straight and narrow, and there is nothing straight, nor is there anything narrow, about nature.

The eye for beauty is the eye for love. We find our beauties in the things that alter nature according to our own visions: in immaculate lawns, in polished pillars of marble, in cornfields, straight as an arrow and clean as a company dinner plate.

We made our way up the mile to the house again. Along the walk in front of it candles had been set out in paper bags full of sand and lighted. The candles gave off a yellow glow like the light of many small campfires, a soft, diffuse, and alluring light. We went in to a potluck supper: fruit salads, vegetable salads, potato salads, hot dishes, cottage pies, fresh-baked loaf breads, orange breads, coffee cakes, other cakes, cookies, a raspberry torte, homemade ice cream, rice pudding, dripped coffee, wine. Eating together is the one biological need we satisfy in company. It is our most natural hour.

After dinner there was talk. Two of the company juggled oranges. There was the singing of Christmas carols. When the last of the carols was done, we were invited to draw into an even closer circle around the potbellied stove and to tell, each one, a story or memory of some Christmas past. It was like the first gathering around a campfire in some cave millennia ago to hear the telling of some other memory. So it was that stories began, and singing and human history. So it was that we began to accumulate the instinct for order. So it was that we began to free ourselves from the here and now, from an eternal entrapment in the present.

It was the circle of little stories into which we were now drawn—the remembrances of food and recitations and customs, of other places and ages—that distinguished us from the prairie world that stretched beyond the dimly lit windows of the old farmhouse into the long night. The ash tree in the yard, and the squirrel that nested in it, and the shelf fungus that was slowly consuming it, and the boxelder bug in the mold at its base, and the stone atop the mold, and the crystal of frost atop the stone, and the star in the heavens above that shone upon them all: each of these beings is forever dependent upon the opportunities of the moment. Each stands before the awesome world now and forever mute.

Inside the farmhouse, we concluded our stories and were offered candles from a straw basket. "Light your candle," the hostess said, "and carry it home with you. If it stays lit the whole way, it will bring you good fortune through the year ahead."

We lit our candles and went away into the winter night. But a little prairie wind had come up, as it always does at evening, and every one of the flames blew out in it. We went away then into our own homes susceptible after all, as is every other creature in the prairie world, to such uncertain opportunities as the next moment and that moment alone might bring.

Suggested Reading

The literature of the prairies is largely the literature of the West, that is, of shortgrass region that extends from the cornbelt to the Rockies. Popular writing about the old tallgrass prairie region, which is the subject of this book, is surprisingly limited, I suppose in the main because it is the story of small towns and of small farms, and because it does not contain the mythic materials of which the cowboys-and-Indians legends of the Wild West were made. Still, it is puzzling that more should not have been written about this region—because the ecosystem itself is a thing of astonishing richness and beauty; because the fertility of this land is to a considerable extent at the economic foundation of the American empire; and because the values and attitudes of the Middle West are woven inextricably into the fabric of American culture.

The imaginative literature of the Middle West is principally protest writing beginning in the teens and twenties, when we were shucking off our agrarian traditions and shaping a new, urban vision of ourselves. Its landmarks are Sinclair Lewis's *Main Street* and Sherwood Anderson's *Winesburg, Ohio* (Penguin, 1976). Still, there are exceptions. Chief among these is O. E. Rolvaag's *Giants in the Earth* (Harper and Row, 1927), which I believe to be one the great American novels. Also notable are the novels of Willa Cather, especially *O, Pioneers!* (Houghton Mifflin, 1974) and *My Antonia* (Houghton Mifflin, 1946). Of particular relevance to this book is the novel *The Chokecherry Tree* by Frederick Manfred (University of New Mexico Press, 1975), which is set in the region I have described.

The two useful introductions to the natural history of the prairie are *The Prairie World* by David Costello (University of Minnesota Press, reprint, 1980) and *Where the Sky Began: Land of the Tallgrass Prairie* by

John Madson (Houghton Mifflin, 1982). Both books have extensive bibliographies and appendixes listing the principal remaining remnants of native prairie. For younger readers, a good introduction is *Tall Grass and Trouble* by Ann E. Sigford, (Dillon Press, 1978). Also indispensable is *A Sand County Almanac* by Aldo Leopold (Oxford University Press, 1966), a passionate plea for an environmental conscience and a book that did as much as any to give birth to the modern-day ecological movement.

Two rewarding books of a more specialized nature are *Watchers at the Pond* by Franklin Russell (Alfred A. Knopf, 1973), a volume with a keener sense of drama, perhaps, than some would find palatable, but still a moving evocation of the teeming life in a prairie marsh; and *Keith County Journal* by John Janovy, Jr. (St. Martin's Press, 1978), a book of considerable charm and irrepressible spirit by a Nebraska biologist, a specialist in parasitology. Janovy succeeds in communicating to general readers the sense of intellectual adventure that a scientist can find, for example, in the natural history of a cowpie.

A fascinating social history of the settlement era on the prairies is *The Sod-House Frontier: 1845–1890* by Everett Dick (University of Nebraska Press, 1979).

Two useful general entries into the vast literature about the native Americans of the prairies are *Indians of the Plains* by Robert H. Lowie (University of Nebraska Press, 1982) and *The Sioux: Life and Customs of a Warrior Society* by Royal B. Hassrick (University of Oklahoma Press, 1964). The book that has most stimulated my own thinking about our cultural attitudes toward the natural world is *Black Elk Speaks* by John G. Neihardt (University of Nebraska Press, 1979).

The great scholarly work about that magnificent symbol of the prairies, the bison, is *The North American Buffalo: A Critical Study of the Species in its Wild State* by F. G. Roe (University of Toronto Press, 1951), and the best of the popular works on the subject is *The Buffalo Book: The Saga of an American Symbol* by David A. Dary (Avon Books, 1974).

Novices interested in exploring the prairie will find *Northland Wild Flowers: A Guide for the Minnesota Region* by John B. and Evelyn W. Moyle (University of Minnesota Press, 1977) a particularly helpful introduction to its plant life. Also very useful, especially for prairie watchers north of the southern boundary of Minnesota, is *Wildflowers of the Northern Great Plains* by F. R. Vance, J. R. Jowsey, and J. S. McLean (University of Minnesota Press, 1984).

About the Author

Paul Gruchow is the author of *Journal of a Prairie Year* (University of Minnesota Press, 1985 & Milkweed Editions, 2009), *The Necessity of Empty Places* (St. Martin's Press, 1988), *Travels in Canoe Country* (Little, Brown, 1992), *Grass Roots* (Milkweed Editions, 1995), and *Boundary Waters* (Milkweed Editions, 1997). Raised in Montevideo, Minnesota, he was educated at the University of Minnesota and worked as the managing editor of the *Worthington Daily Globe*. Prior to his death in 2004, Paul taught at St. Olaf College and Concordia College, and was a frequent contributor to the *Utne Reader*, the *New York Times*, and the *Hungry Mind Review*, among other publications.

Acknowledgments

I am indebted to Marjorie Fader, who first encouraged me to think of myself as a writer; to Jim Brandenburg, who first taught me to see the prairie; to my business partners, James L. Vance and Owen Van Essen, who granted me a generous leave of absence at a critical stage in the writing of this manuscript; to my wife, Nancy, who never questioned the long absences the work entailed, even when she was baffled by my enthusiasm for the subject; to Katie Murphy, who typed the manuscript many times, and who told me when it was confusing; to William A. Wood of the University of Minnesota Press, who offered exactly the sort of gentle encouragement and criticism that every author prays for; to Victoria Haire, also of the Press, whose sharp and sympathetic editing made the book better in literally hundreds of ways; and to Joe Rossi, who shared many of the experiences in the book during our stimulating collaboration as writer and photographer.

Portions of this book first appeared, in earlier drafts, in *Minnesota Monthly*, *Great River Review*, *The Loonfeather*, the anthology *The Minnesota Experience*, and the *Worthington Daily Globe*.

More Books from Milkweed Editions

To order books or for more information, contact Milkweed
at (800) 520-6455 or visit our Web site (www.milkweed.org).

Boundary Waters
Paul Gruchow

Grass Roots
Paul Gruchow

The Future of Nature:
Writing on a Human Ecology from Orion Magazine
Selected and Introduced by Barry Lopez

Shopping for Porcupine: A Life in Arctic Alaska
Seth Kantner

The Windows of Brimnes: An American in Iceland
Bill Holm

Milkweed Editions

Founded in 1979, Milkweed Editions is one of the largest independent, nonprofit literary publishers in the United States. Milkweed publishes with the intention of making a humane impact on society, in the belief that good writing can transform the human heart and spirit.

Join Us

Milkweed depends on the generosity of foundations and individuals like you, in addition to the sales of its books. In an increasingly consolidated and bottom-line-driven publishing world, your support allows us to select and publish books on the basis of their literary quality and the depth of their message. Please visit our Web site (www.milkweed. org) or contact us at (800) 520-6455 to learn more about our donor program.

Milkweed Editions, a nonprofit publisher, gratefully acknowledges sustaining support from Anonymous; Emilie and Henry Buchwald; the Patrick and Aimee Butler Family Foundation; the Dougherty Family Foundation; the Ecolab Foundation; the General Mills Foundation; the Claire Giannini Fund; John and Joanne Gordon; William and Jeanne Grandy; the Jerome Foundation; Constance and Daniel Kunin; the Lerner Foundation; Sanders and Tasha Marvin; the McKnight Foundation; Mid-Continent Engineering; the Minnesota State Arts Board, through an appropriation by the Minnesota State Legislature, a grant from the Wells Fargo Foundation Minnesota, and a grant from the National Endowment for the Arts; Kelly Morrison and John Willoughby; the National Endowment for the Arts; the Navarre Corporation; Ann and Doug Ness; Ellen Sturgis; the Target Foundation; the James R. Thorpe Foundation; the Travelers Foundation; Moira and John Turner; Joanne and Phil Von Blon; Kathleen and Bill Wanner; and the W. M. Foundation.

MINNESOTA
STATE ARTS BOARD

NATIONAL
ENDOWMENT
FOR THE ARTS
A great nation
deserves great art.

TARGET.

THE M^CKNIGHT FOUNDATION

Interior design by Connie Kuhnz
Typeset in Goudy Old Style
by BookMobile Design and Publishing Services, Minneapolis, MN
Printed on acid-free, recycled (100% post consumer waste),
   Rolland paper
by Friesens Corporation